The Project Management Advisor:

18 Major Project Screw-ups, and How to Cut Them off at the Pass

Lonnie Pacelli

PRENTICE HALL
An Imprint of PEARSON EDUCATION
Upper Saddle River, NJ • London • San Francisco • Toronto • Sydney
Tokyo • Singapore • Hong Kong • Cape Town • Madrid
Paris • Milan • Munich • Amsterdam
www.ftp-ph.com

A CIP record of this book can be obtained from the Libary of Congress.

Publisher: *Tim Moore*
Acquisitions Editor: *Paula Sinnott*
Editorial Assistant: *Rick Winkler*
Marketing Manager: *Martin Litkowski*
International Marketing Manager: *Tim Galligan*
Managing Editor: *Gina Kanouse*
Production and Interior Design: *Specialized Composition , Inc.*
Cover Design: *Anthony Gemmellaro*
Manufacturing Buyer: *Dan Uhrig*

 © 2004 Pearson Education, Inc.
Publishing as Prentice Hall
Upper Saddle River, New Jersey 07458

Prentice Hall offers excellent discounts on this book when ordered in quantity for bulk purchases or special sales. For more information, please contact: U.S. Corporate and Government Sales, 1-800-382-3419, corpsales@pearsontech-group.com. For sales outside of the United States, please contact: International Sales, 1-317-581-3793, international@pearsontechgroup.com.

Company and product names mentioned herein are the trademarks or registered trademarks of their respective owners.

Printed in the United States of America

First Printing

ISBN 0131490478

Pearson Education Ltd.
Pearson Education Australia Pty., Limited
Pearson Education Singapore, Pte. Ltd.
Pearson Education North Asia Ltd.
Pearson Education Canada, Ltd.
Pearson Educación de Mexico, S.A. de C.V.
Pearson Education—Japan
Pearson Education Malaysia, Pte. Ltd.

Contents at a Glance

Preface

Acknowledgements

Screw-up #1 – We weren't addressing the right problem
Screw-up #2—We designed the wrong thing
Screw-up #3—We used the wrong technology
Screw-up #4—We didn't design a good project schedule
Screw-up #5—We didn't have the right sponsorship
Screw-up #6—The team didn't gel
Screw-up #7—We didn't involve the right people
Screw-up #8—We didn't communicate what we were doing
Screw-up #9—We didn't pay attention to project risks and management issues
Screw-up #10—The project cost much more than expected
Screw-up #11—We didn't understand and report progress against the plan
Screw-up #12—We tried to do too much
Screw-up #13—We didn't do enough testing
Screw-up #14—We weren't effective at training the customer
Screw-up #15—We didn't pull the plug on the project when we should have
Screw-up #16—We tripped at the finish line
Screw-up #17—The vendor didn't deliver
Screw-up #18—We had no fallback position in case the product failed
Wrapping It Up...

Table of Contents

Preface

Acknowledgements

Screw-up #1   We weren't addressing
the right problem   1

HOW IT HAPPENS   2
    There's a poorly articulated mission statement   2
    There's an inconsistent understanding of
    what the problem is   3
    It's a problem but there are bigger fish to fry   4

WARNING SIGNS   5
    You are having difficulty getting a sponsor
    for your project   5
    The project team is confused about what
    problem the project is trying to address   5
    It is difficult to keep the project team focused
    on solving the problem   5

TURNING IT AROUND   6
    Keep your mission statement prominently displayed   6
    Adjust the mission if the problem changes   6
    Put it on hold   6

TAKE AWAYS   7

Screw-up #2 We Designed the Wrong Thing 9

HOW IT HAPPENS 10
The project isn't scoped correctly 10
The customer is not adequately involved
in the design process 13
The project team was under pressure to start doing
"real work," such as implementing the design 14
Something is lost in interpretation between
requirements and design 15
A bad process is automated to do something
bad faster 16
There is a poor or non-existent design
change process 17

WARNING SIGNS 18
There's no "voice of the customer" on the project 18
The project team customers can't see beyond
how things are done today 18
The customers are continually confused as to how
they're going to do their job under the new design 19
The new design keeps changing late into the project 19
The customers lose interest in the project and
stop participating 19

TURNING THINGS AROUND 19
Right-size customer involvement 19
Listen to the customer 20
Slow down or stop the project to ensure that
the design is going to meet business needs 20
Keep true to your scope 20

TAKE AWAYS 21

Screw-up #3 We Used the Wrong Technology 23

HOW IT HAPPENS 24
The technology is not time tested 24
The technology does not meet the business
functionality need 25

There are inexperienced people working with
the technology 26

The technology isn't able to handle the volumes
of the business 26

WARNING SIGNS 27

The technology keeps failing during your project 27

You hear "it's in the next release" too much 27

Your customers keep complaining about
the technology 27

Your project team members who are responsible
for the technology are taking longer than expected
to fix problems 27

TURNING IT AROUND 28

Test the technology until you're comfortable
it's going to work 28

Get the right skills to work on and develop
the technology 28

Stop while it's still containable 28

TAKE AWAYS 29

Screw-up #4 We Didn't Design a Good
Project Schedule 31

HOW IT HAPPENS 32

The project schedule was either too detailed
or not detailed enough 32

The project schedule doesn't correctly address
dependencies between tasks 34

The project duration is too long 34

Some of the tasks doesn't produce useful
deliverables 35

The team doesn't understand the plan 35

WARNING SIGNS 36

Tasks aren't getting done on time 36

Tasks assigned to "the team" or some other group
of people aren't getting done 36

Team members aren't aware that they are
supposed to be working on a task 36

Team members are confused as to what they
are supposed to produce for a task   36

TURNING IT AROUND   37

Get real with the schedule, and fast   37

Do focused reviews with team members   37

Keep dependencies simple   37

Highlight tasks that are due in the next 1-2 weeks   38

TAKE AWAYS   38

Screw-up #5   We Didn't Have the Right Sponsorship   39

HOW IT HAPPENS   42

The project sponsor is either too high or too
low in the organization   42

The project sponsor is being inundated with
issues that could be resolved by a steering
committee   42

You make the project sponsor work too hard to
try to understand your project   43

You don't tell the project sponsor what you need   44

You meet either too much or not enough with your
project sponsor   44

WARNING SIGNS   45

You don't have an identified project sponsor   45

You can't get the project sponsor's attention   45

Your project sponsor doesn't help you with
management issues   45

TURNING THINGS AROUND   46

Make sure that your project sponsor is
current and engaged   46

Clarify your project sponsor's expectations   46

Right-size your time with your
project sponsor   46

Tell your project sponsor explicitly what you need
for the project to succeed   46

Strongly consider stopping the project   47

TAKE AWAYS   47

Screw-up #6 The Team Didn't Gel   49

HOW IT HAPPENS   50
There is not a clear project organization
with clearly defined roles   50
The team finger points and fights in public   51
There is no "rallying cry"   52
Team members aren't held accountable for delivery   53
The project manager isn't suited for the job   54
The team doesn't celebrate wins   55

WARNING SIGNS   55
The team shows confusion about who is doing what   55
Discussions are destructive and unproductive   56
Team members aren't helping each other   56

TURNING IT AROUND   56
Clarify the confusion   56
Address the problem team member   56
Co-locate the team   57
Go out for a milkshake   57
All work and no play…   57
Be the unifier   57

TAKE AWAYS   58

Screw-up #7 We Didn't Involve the Right People 59

HOW IT HAPPENS   61
There is not clear definition on who the customer is 61
Others who could help with specific issues on
the project aren't utilized   61
The people who can torpedo a project aren't
identified and managed   62

WARNING SIGNS   62
You're getting a lot of questions from other
stakeholder groups on what you're doing   62
Uninvited stakeholders start showing up at
project meetings   63
Project issues are taking longer than expected
to resolve   63

TURNING IT AROUND   63

  Communicate, communicate, communicate   63

  Know whom to call   63

  Right-size project involvement   64

  Let your project sponsor help you   64

  Be open to adjusting the focus and scope of
  the project   64

TAKE AWAYS   65

Screw-up #8   We Didn't Communicate What We
Were Doing   67

HOW IT HAPPENS   71

  Audiences are not defined clearly   71

  You create a great communication plan but it
  isn't followed   71

  The communication isn't tuned to the audience   71

  The communication doesn't come from the
  right person   72

WARNING SIGNS   72

  Your audience asks questions about the project that
  you've already communicated   72

  You're getting a lot of one-off requests for project
  information from audiences not in your
  communication plan   73

  Your audience requests go unanswered   73

TURNING IT AROUND   73

  Right-size the communication to the audiences   73

  Take some time to redefine your audiences
  and how to communicate with them   74

  Follow the plan   74

  Make requests explicit and easy to see   74

TAKE AWAYS   74

Screw-up #9 We Didn't Pay Attention to Project
Risks and Management Issues   75

HOW IT HAPPENS   78

Project risks or management issues don't get
defined or don't focus on the important stuff   78

Project risks are defined but there is no mitigation
strategy to manage through the risk   79

Management issues are documented but there's no
defined action to manage through the issues   80

WARNING SIGNS   80

You don't have a project risk or issue list   80

You don't have a plan for how you would
mitigate risks from coming true   80

There's no clear owner or need date for
resolving issues   81

The project sponsor or steering
committee isn't utilized effectively for resolving issues 81

TURNING IT AROUND   81

Get your risks defined and define clear mitigation
strategies for each risk   81

Right-size the issue list   82

Know who's on the hook   82

TAKE AWAYS   82

Screw-up #10 The Project Cost Much More Than
Expected   83

HOW IT HAPPENS   86

The project estimate at completion variance
isn't managed   86

The project actual resource mix is different from
the budgeted resource mix   86

The project doesn't plan for or manage a
contingency fund   86

The project manager's request for additional
funding isn't credible   87

WARNING SIGNS 88

Your current variance keeps growing as the
project goes on 88

You have to do more unplanned work than
you originally anticipated 88

You don't know how much contingency
you've consumed and what it was consumed on 88

Your current variance fluctuates but your estimate to
complete variance stays at zero 89

TURNING IT AROUND 89

Get a grip on your cost situation 89

Understand what tradeoffs you can make on
remaining work 89

Minimize the number of times you ask for
more money 90

TAKE AWAYS 90

Screw-up #11   We Didn't Understand and Report
Progress Against the Plan 91

HOW IT HAPPENS 100

Progress against the schedule isn't tracked
or is not kept up to date 100

Weekly team meetings aren't held 100

Status reports aren't prepared or aren't timely 101

Action isn't taken quickly when problems
cropped up 101

WARNING SIGNS 102

You're getting questions about the progress of
the project from stakeholders or team members 102

The project team isn't clear on the problems that
the project is currently facing 102

Problems don't have a clear owner or "resolution
needed-by" date 102

You don't know when something is about to
be a problem 102

TURNING IT AROUND   103
  Get real with the schedule   103
  Listen for trains   103
  Keep it simple   103
  Get trackin'   104

TAKE AWAYS   104

Screw-up #12   We Tried to Do Too Much   105

HOW IT HAPPENS   108
  Project scope isn't set or controlled appropriately   108
  The project team doesn't know when to say
  'good enough'   108
  The team attempts to fill available hours of
  capacity with additional work   109

WARNING SIGNS   109
  You hear too many "it would be great if the
  product did…" after product design is frozen   109
  The project team is working too many hours   109
  There's confusion about the scope of the
  project after product design is frozen   110

TURNING IT AROUND   110
  Lock down the scope   110
  Know when to say no   110
  Revise the project schedule and budget to
  accommodate change in scope   111

TAKE AWAYS   111

Screw-up #13   We Didn't Do Enough Testing   113

HOW IT HAPPENS   115
  There is no test plan   115
  There is a plan but it isn't being followed   116
  There isn't a clear definition of what
  success means   116
  The customer isn't included in the testing   117
  The project team "assumes" something
  will work   117

WARNING SIGNS 118
Product testing is starting later than planned 118
Your customer is finding problems that your
internal project team should have found 118
Testing is scheduled to be complete but product
success criteria hasn't been met 118

TURNING IT AROUND 119
Pull testing back to earlier phase
and re-test 119
Get the team focused on a deadline 119
Stop testing if there are a lot of product problems
that are blocking you from continuing testing 119

TAKE AWAYS 120

Screw-up #14 We Weren't Effective at
Training the Customer 121

HOW IT HAPPENS 123
It's not clear who needs to be trained on what 123
The training is too product focused
and doesn't put the product in context of
the business and policy changes 123
The project team develops the wrong type
of training 124
There are too many presentation slides and
not enough hands-on training with the product 125
The trainers understand the product, but not
the business 125
The product keeps failing while trying to train the
customers 126

WARNING SIGNS 126
Customers aren't attending the training 126
Trainers aren't able to address business
usage issues 126
After attending the training,
customers still don't get it 127

TURNING IT AROUND 127

Make the training targeted, relevant, and timely 127

Do a practice training session 127

Assign your customer project team members to
participate in delivering the training 127

Get immediate feedback on the quality of the
training 128

Stop the training and re-design 128

TAKE AWAYS 128

Screw-up #15   We Didn't Pull the Plug on the
Project When We Should Have 129

HOW IT HAPPENS 131

There are no specific checkpoints
established to ensure that the project should
proceed 131

The team is emotionally tied to the project 131

The team relies on a silver bullet to save a
sick project 132

WARNING SIGNS 132

The customer or project sponsor loses interest
in the project 132

The project sponsor changes 133

There are major outstanding issues that can kill
the project 133

There's skepticism about the
viability of the project's business case 133

TURNING IT AROUND 134

Define checkpoint milestones to
confirm project continuation 134

Assess the outstanding major issues to determine
if continuing is the right answer 134

Stop the project 134

TAKE AWAYS 134

Screw-up #16   We Tripped at the Finish Line   135

HOW IT HAPPENS   136

Someone implements a last-minute product
change that breaks something else   136

Project communication among the team isn't
timely   137

The project starts shutting down prior to
completion   137

WARNING SIGNS   138

Team members are being re-assigned to other
projects   138

Customers are demanding last-minute
non-essential product changes   138

Project team communications have dropped
off or are non-existent   138

TURNING IT AROUND   139

Keep the focus   139

Drive the team to communicate   139

Stabilize the product   139

TAKE AWAYS   140

Screw-up #17   The Vendor Didn't Deliver   141

HOW IT HAPPENS   143

The vendor oversells their product or
capabilities   143

There isn't a clear agreement on what the
vendor is supposed to do   144

The customer doesn't live up to their
obligations   144

The vendor does a "bait and switch" with resources   145

The vendor isn't treated like part of the team   145

The vendor is over- or under-managed by
the project manager   146

WARNING SIGNS   147

   The vendor keeps slipping their scheduled dates   147

   The vendor is rolling people off of the
   project earlier than anticipated   147

   The vendor spends time trying to sell
   additional work using their project team members   147

   The vendor's deliverables aren't meeting your
   expectations   148

   The vendor has staffed the project with
   inexperienced people   148

TURNING IT AROUND   148

   Address the people skill sets issue   148

   Manage to more detailed, frequent
   milestones   148

   Contain the vendor   149

   Make sure that the vendor has skin in the game   149

   Replace the vendor   149

TAKE AWAYS   149

Screw-up #18   We Had No Fallback Position
in Case the Product Failed   151

HOW IT HAPPENS   154

   There is no contingency plan in place   154

   There is a contingency plan, but it isn't followed   154

   Project management does not stay engaged
   through the implementation   155

WARNING SIGNS   155

   The customer is asking questions about what
   happens if the new product
   implementation isn't successful   155

   The project team doesn't know what it needs to
   do in the event of an unsuccessful implementation   155

TURNING IT AROUND   156

   Get the contingency plan scenarios down   156

   Test the plan   156

   Go back to the old product, fix the new, and then
   re-release   156

TAKE AWAYS   157

Wrapping It up...   159

Index 161

Preface

Any of these sound familiar?

- A critical project task that quickly gets to 90% complete and takes forever to get the last 10% done
- You're about to release your product and a stakeholder that wasn't involved in the design jumps up and down and causes significant product rework
- Your project team spends more time fighting and finger-pointing than working together to get the project done

As an experienced project manager, chances are you've lived through some of these situations at least once and can probably add several of your own bullets to the list. If so, I think you'll enjoy *The Project Management Advisor*.

In my 20 years' experience in running projects as a consultant, project manager, and business owner, I'm proud to say that I've experienced many project successes. But strangely enough, it's the screw-ups that stick at the forefront of my mind, and it's those projects that I think about whenever I'm starting up a new project. I'm bound and determined not to repeat mistakes that I've made on prior projects. I so clearly remember that touching a hot stove hurts just as much the second time as it did the first time. Nonetheless, I've been back to that stove numerous times over the years…and have the scars to prove it!

As a fellow project management practitioner, I wanted to write a book specifically for the experienced project manager who understands the fundamentals of project management but would benefit from tips on how to make projects more successful. In writing this book, I wanted to design it as something that a project manager doesn't just read once and put on a shelf to forever gather dust. I wanted to design it so that you could refer back to it time and time again depending on the specific challenges that you are facing on your particular project.

Each chapter of the book focuses on a common project screw-up to help you avoid some of the wasted time, pain, and expense that inevitably comes with a failed project. Each chapter is organized with icons to help you navigate the chapter and find things quickly.

 icon is used wherever I explain why the screw-up occurs.

 icon is used wherever I explain the warning signs that you should be looking for which signal that a screw-up is approaching.

 icon is used wherever I explain what you could do to turn the situation around if you start seeing warning signs.

icon is used to summarize key points for you to remember from the chapter.

In addition to being an experienced practitioner, I am also an eager student of the art of project management and have found that I've learned something from every project that I've participated in or lead. I'd love to hear what you have to say about the tips in this book, where they have helped you, what war stories you've been through, and also where you disagree with me. Tell me what you think by going to my website at www.projectmanagementadvisor.com and telling me your story.

I sincerely hope that you enjoy *The Project Management Advisor* as much as I enjoyed writing it. Surely some of the project screw-ups will resonate with you, and I hope that you are able to take away some helpful nuggets that you are able to use in your projects.

Acknowledgements

Throughout my career at both Accenture and Microsoft, there have been a number of people that have molded, shaped, and influenced me and have been instrumental in helping me to be a better project manager. From Accenture, Bob Frerichs, Steve Foreman, Drew Blanchard, Jack Levy, Ed Motley, Kent Swanson, Mitch Hill, and Bill Schaffner were tremendous influences and great role models. From Microsoft, Craig Bruya, Nick MacPhee, Scott Boggs, Mike Huber, John Connors, and Taylor Hawes helped me to take what I learned at Accenture and apply it in a very practical manner.

In writing this book, I first and foremost owe a special debt of gratitude to David Dwyer, who gave me some very wise counsel on how to best go about writing a book and helped me to hook up with my publisher to make the book possible. I also want to thank Clayton Fleming, Dale Christian, Arun Kumar, Louie Gracey, Jim Thomas, Kent Kading, Leo Ahearn, David Gill, Darren Ellis, Gil Wootton, Michael VanFossen, Lou Pacelli, Barney Kinzer and Pete Peterson for their very thorough reviews of the book and for their wise counsel on how to make the book more relevant for project managers as a whole.

Special thanks to Paula Sinnott, Acquiring Editor at Prentice Hall, for her tireless energy and enduring patience with me as we fine-tuned the book, and for making this such a pleasurable experience for me. I also want to send a sincere thanks to the production team for their diligence in making this book a reality and for guiding me through the publishing process, especially Gina Kanouse, Managing Editor at Pearson, and Specialized Composition, Inc. for editing and production.

Last but not least, I want to thank my wonderful wife, Patty for her support of me writing the book, for proofreading revisions, and for being patient with me while I worked late at night and early in the mornings on manuscript revisions. I also want to thank my children, Briana and Trevor, for being such awesome kids and helping me to keep my priorities straight.

We Weren't Addressing the Right Problem

Virtually every (rational) project has at its core a need to solve some problem that is perceived by someone. Problems can manifest themselves as barriers to getting something done ("We can't possibly ship 10,000 units/week with our existing systems") or as opportunity to do something better ("We need to reduce the cost of processing purchase orders by 20%"). In any event, there is a desire to do something tomorrow that can't be achieved today.

Admittedly, some of the most fun projects that I have worked on have been the "Omigosh, we need to get this done or else" projects. I have seen the greatest clarity of purpose on projects where there was a very real and tangible consequence to not completing the project successfully. One outstanding example of this that affected virtually every business on earth was the Y2K computer scare. One of my jobs was ensuring that our mission-critical vendors were adequately prepared for Y2K and that there would not be any business interruption to our company as a result of a vendor's failure to perform. Everyone knew what the problem was: computer systems that only used a two-digit year and assumed that the "19" in the first two years were going to assume a year of "1900" on January 1, 2000 and, depending on the system, everything from power grids to air traffic systems to small appliances had the potential to malfunction. You all know the story: 1/1/2000 came and went with a minimum of problems; not because the scare was overblown, but because there were billions of dollars spent worldwide ensuring that a problem didn't occur. There was tremendous clarity of purpose and a very real and tangible consequence if no action had been taken.

 # HOW IT HAPPENS

There's a poorly articulated mission statement

Many projects that I have seen had a mission statement that was either vague, unrealistic, or simply didn't exist. Saying, "We need to reduce costs" is admirable and desirable, but is not something a project team can surgically execute simply because it is not clear what the project is and when the project will be complete.

The best mission statements that I have seen have the following components:

- What needs to be done

- When it needs to be done

- What measure will be used to evaluate success

One project that I worked on focused on vendors entering invoices directly into a company's invoicing system via the Internet as opposed to invoicing via a hardcopy document. The mission statement for the project was as follows:

> **"We need to reduce the cost of processing invoices by 50% by March 1, while ensuring that vendors are paid within terms 100% of the time."**

The project had a clear *what* (reduce the cost of processing invoices), a clear *when* (March 1) and clear *measure* (50% cost of processing and 100% of the time payment within terms). In the invoicing project, we were able to stay laser-focused on what we needed to do and make sure that all the project constituents stayed in sync because we had a super-focused mission statement.

There's an inconsistent understanding of what the problem is

On projects where you have multiple stakeholder groups, there is a very strong likelihood that each stakeholder group is going to have a specific agenda that they bring to the project. Some may view what you perceive to be the problem as not being a problem at all. Very early on in your project, it is crucial to get a very consistent view of what the project is intended to accomplish via the use of the clear mission statement and ensure that the constituents understand the mission and are bought into working to resolve it.

At times you're going to have the "resisters" who don't want to complete the project because it means significant change or elimination of their job or organization. It is vital to address this early in the mission statement definition and to identify the concerns of the resister. One technique that I have used with success is to get the stakeholders in a room and to give them each an opportunity to somehow shape the mission statement. What I have found is that even if someone only adds or changes *one word* of the mission statement they feel that they have influenced the direction of the project.

On some projects, we've been able to turn some of the resisters around; on others, the resisters never got with the game plan. In those instances, the resister ultimately was taken off the project. It's never a smooth process to remove a resister, but it's always been necessary to keep the project moving forward.

It's a problem but there are bigger fish to fry

So, maybe you see something that isn't working as well as it should be, or you see some product or service that could benefit your organization. It very well could be that implementing the solution could reap some benefit to your organization; the questions become those of management priorities and focus.

In one organization I worked with, we developed an annual portfolio of projects that identified the project, the problem the project was addressing, the resource needs, the benefit expected, a subjective priority of the project based on management priority and focus, and the duration that the project was to take. After each project definition was completed, we put the projects in a spreadsheet, sorted the projects by priority, and did a "draw the line" series of meetings based on when resources would be consumed. As an example, if we got to a point where after five projects there were no more dollars available to work on projects, we "drew the line" after the fifth project. I'd be kidding you if I said this was purely an arithmetic exercise and everyone walked away doing cartwheels over the outcome. The process forces a lot of discussion on relative priorities and, while one organization may feel that a project is vitally important to their business, in the larger scheme of things there were projects that were more important. So, not everyone was thrilled with the outcome, but there was a prioritized project list that everyone knew and understood.

Now, things do change and the relative priorities of projects do change. Thus, it's important that the project list is reviewed periodically (we did it quarterly) to ensure that you're still working on the right things in the right priority sequence.

 # WARNING SIGNS

You are having difficulty getting a sponsor for your project

So you've got a project that you think is important but you're having a difficult time convincing potential sponsors that the problem is significant enough that they should care and take action. It could be that the problem is truly legitimate but it's not a high enough priority to warrant immediate action. Then again, it also could mean that you've got a poorly defined mission statement that isn't compelling enough to take action.

The project team is confused about what problem the project is trying to address

I've seen more than one project where the project team goes through the project with different views about what problem needs to be solved. If each of your project team members is unable to consistently recite your mission statement, you're sure to have points of confusion throughout your project.

It is difficult to keep the project team focused on solving the problem

On some projects, I have encountered situations where project team members stray from solving the root problem to solving a "problem du jour" which may or may not be related to the project. At times, there could be validity to the issue being raised, and it might help you to further articulate your problem statement and resulting solution. At other times, though, it could just be a red herring that dilutes your focus and creates confusion about what you're trying to accomplish.

TURNING IT AROUND

Keep your mission statement prominently displayed

I've seen some projects where there's a great mission statement that is developed in order to sell the project, and then it's put in a drawer for no one to see ever again. Ensure that you are re-visiting and re-communicating the mission statement through-out the life of the project to ensure that you're doing the right thing, that everyone understands what the right thing is, and that you're driving toward resolving the problem.

Adjust the mission if the problem changes

Problems aren't immutable; they can change in complexity and importance. If something changes about the problem, make sure that your mission changes accordingly. This could also mean that the importance of your project changes because the problem is either more or less important than it was prior to the change.

Put it on hold

If you can't get support for the project, either put it on hold or recognize that it's not something that sponsors care enough to address at the present time. Better you do this than try to forge ahead with the project without sponsorship. It's likely only a matter of time before the project dies.

 **TAKE AWAYS**

- Make sure that you've got a very clearly articulated mission statement

- Ensure that your key stakeholders understand the mission statement and have had an opportunity to tweak it

- Make sure that the mission statement is in line with potential sponsor priorities and focus, and prioritized appropriately with other projects

- Prominently display the mission statement for your team

We Designed
the Wrong Thing

On most projects—whether you're building a system, an automobile, or a skyscraper—you start with a design of how it will look. In building this design, you take into account what the end customer finds desirable in the product and what can be done given any constraints placed on the project to come up with your final solution. The more effectively you can involve your end customer in your design, the better likelihood of an overall project success.

Too often, though, project teams rush through the design process only to find out later that key features important to the customer are either designed incorrectly or missing altogether. I've been on too many projects where an end product was released to the customer only to find out that a key feature that should have been designed into the product was flat out missing. Aside from the stress on the team to recover from the design omission, the project takes a public relations hit for missing a key feature. Very frustrating, indeed.

 **HOW IT HAPPENS**

The project isn't scoped correctly

As an end customer (when I say "customer," I am referring to the primary beneficiary of the project), there are four little words that, when heard, are like waving a red flag in front of a bull: *it's out of scope*. In my experience both on the giving and receiving end of this phrase, the discussion immediately following these four little words can be fairly frustrating and destructive. I can also guarantee you that on any project that you do you will at some time have to use those words to keep the project on track and not get distracted.

In scoping your project, it's important to define your scope statement very early in the design process. Some of the best scope statements that I have seen on projects look at scope from the following dimensions:

- The *functional* scope of the project; in other words, "What business processes are to be included in the design?"

- The *geographical* scope of the project; for example, "Will the design be implemented in one location, region, country, or worldwide?"

- The *organizational* scope of the project; in other words, "Will the design affect the department, the division, or the entire company?"

- Specific *exceptions* to scope; for example, "What items will specifically be excluded from scope that, unless they're called out, would be assumed to be in scope?"

When developing a scope statement, I like to test the scope statement's reasonableness by asking some basic questions:

- How many decision makers will have to weigh in on project decisions?

- Can I reasonably divide the scope into phases or does it all need to be done at once?

- Can I focus on fewer (or one) organizations first and then do others after the first one is done?

My dream projects have a single decision maker on the project, can be broken up neatly into logical phases, and allow me to focus on a small control group in the first phase and then on other organizations and geographies in subsequent phases. When you're able to control those variables and the scope correctly, life on the project can be great.

Sometimes as a project manager you're able to define things so clearly, but at other times you're simply handed a problem that doesn't give this flexibility. On one project that I led we were given the assignment of implementing a new process and system which needed to support an annual business planning process. Some immutable requirements needed to be satisfied: the system needed to be global, support every organization required to do this type of planning, meet very specific customer requirements, include several key decision makers, and be done by a certain date or else the entire company planning process would be impacted. As these client needs were being explained to me, I envisioned the old "Mission Impossible" TV series where each episode started with the assignment explained via reel-to-reel tape followed by a "should you accept this assignment" statement and climaxing with the tape self-destructing after five seconds. So, of all the things that I like to have when defining project scope, I got exactly *none* of them. Nonetheless, because it was crucial to the business and because we had a very motivated executive sponsor, we executed the project using very tight scope and milestone management and it was a tremendous success.

In defining your scope statement, it's important to ensure that the end customers, executive sponsor, and the project team are clear on where the boundary lines have been drawn. Now, here is where I make a distinction between a marginal project manager and a great project manager:

- A *marginal* project manager draws the boundaries in permanent marker and either will not waver under any circumstances as the design is fleshed out or will completely ignore the boundaries and accept scope changes without understanding project impacts.

- A *great* project manager draws the lines in pencil and is very deliberate in deciding when lines need to be redrawn to better meet business needs while understanding the impacts to the project.

As you are fleshing out your design, you need to clearly know where you've drawn the boundaries but be cognizant of where a boundary has been drawn incorrectly. After your design is frozen and you're in change-control mode, you can draw the boundaries in darker ink but you still need to know when you're doing the wrong thing because of the boundaries you've drawn. More importantly, you need to know the tradeoffs that need to be made (additional funds, time, or resources) and propose a sound resolution. On one project that I led we were one week from releasing the product to the customers when our product manager realized that a key usability feature was omitted and, if implemented, would have significantly degraded the customer's overall experience. Our development manager was adamant that we should not implement the feature as it seemed too risky and could negatively impact other product features. In looking at the problem from a risk, time, cost, and customer experience perspective, we decided to implement the change but did it in a very controlled, tightly managed process that allowed us to ensure that the change would work without negatively impacting other features of the product. We were able to successfully implement the change without impacting the overall release and avoided negative repercussions with our customers.

The customer is not adequately involved in the design process

With every project success, there has always been appropriate access to credible, critical-thinking, rational customers. The best customer project team members that I've seen displayed the following traits:

- They represented their area completely and took responsibility for pulling in other subject matter experts as needed.

- They were able to make reasonable tradeoffs on functionality when necessary.

- They were open to new ways of doing things and actively tried to make their business process better.

- They were well respected by their home organization.

- They were willing to be "one of the team" and work side-by-side with the development teams to ensure that nothing got lost between design and implementation.

For these traits to be realized, the customer needs to be viewed by the project team as an insider and needs to be actively listened to when they are defining their needs. That's not to say that the customer should come down from the mountain with their requirements etched in stone tablets while the rest of the team stands in awe of the customer's omniscience. It is very healthy for team members to critically question the customer and each other on how to make something work better regardless of automation. Some of the best ideas I've seen in business designs have been when someone that is removed from the process is able to ask childlike "why" questions. This can only happen effectively if you get the customer plugged in early.

A common question arises when trying to identify customers: How many and for how long? Unfortunately, there's no one-size-fits-all answer. The best projects I've seen have used as few customers as possible to provide the greatest functional coverage. I'd much rather have one dedicated customer that embodies the traits identified previously that has 80% of the functional coverage than five part-time customer specialists that together make up 100% functional coverage. Here's why:

- There are fewer people on the project that the project manager has to manage

- There is less confusion amongst project team members about the customers that they need to be working with

- There is no competition for how much of the customer's time that the project team gets because the customer is dedicated to the project; part-time resources are more likely to get pulled back to their primary jobs

- The full-time customer has a bigger-picture view of the entire process and will be better able to see implications of decisions across the entire process, as opposed to focusing on a smaller area

The project team is under pressure to start doing "real work," such as implementing the design

I've seen this happen numerous times on projects and in every instance it boiled down to one of two reasons: stakeholder project expectations or the project team not knowing when to finish the design and start development. With stakeholder project expectations, the customers, project manager, or executive sponsor feels that the solution is "simple" and that they should be able to "just start implementing." In an effort to please the stakeholder, the project team accepts the feedback and plunges into development. With this, though, the developers are left to interpret details that would otherwise be specified by the customer. This could work if you've got business-savvy developers, but typically that is the exception to the rule.

On the flip side, the project team could have an elongated design phase that completes all the design documentation with a high degree of precision prior to starting any development. While the design documentation could be quite thorough, the project loses momentum because the team and management don't see a solution to their business problem being solved quickly enough.

I've seen the best success on this problem when the project team briskly moves through the design process, sets very deliberate completion milestones, and is able to frequently show progress on the design via prototypes, which I'll get into in more depth in the next section.

Something is lost in interpretation between requirements and design

In many projects, a "customer requirements document" is completed which documents in detail the customer's needs to be served by the project at hand. The customer would then be asked to stick their fingers and sign in blood that these requirements are true, complete, and accurate. The requirements would then be used in developing a product design, which is then translated into an implemented solution. In my role as a business owner, I have always found it extremely difficult to stare at a requirements document and certify that this is the complete population of requirements that I am expecting the system to satisfy. Also, I would be forced to think about it in terms of my "as-is" world and not in a better "to-be" world. Pretty tough stuff.

Over the years I've become a huge fan of rapid prototyping as a means to flesh out requirements, particularly on systems projects. In rapid prototyping, the project team agrees on the business processes that need to be addressed or the problems that need to be solved. Then, the customer is paired with a developer bunked together in a cubicle, conference room, or office and does screen-by-screen prototypes of what a system would need to do to satisfy the business process. During prototyping, the sole focus is on mirroring as closely as possible how the business system's functionality would satisfy requirements at its completion and allowing the customer to envision doing their job using the new system. As the prototype matures, the customer shops it around to peer end customers and other stakeholders to review the process and get feedback on how to make it better. The end result is a rich functional model of how the new business process and system will work in terms that a customer can easily understand and picture.

In its final form, the prototype serves multiple purposes. First, it serves as a working model that developers can use in technical design and development. Second, it serves as a model for testers and trainers to develop their respective plans. Third, it is a great sales vehicle for the customer to review with other customers in terms of what the new system is going to be able to do to make their lives easier. Fourth, it is a rich deliverable that can be easily demonstrated to the executive sponsor and key stakeholders to show project progress and generate excitement for the new system.

A bad process is automated to do something bad faster

If your project requires redesigning processes, it is always good to take a hard look at the processes and make sure that worthless activities are removed as the design is completed. There is a myriad of techniques that you can use (such as six-sigma) to discover inefficiencies. Regardless of the technique used, your goal is simplicity and clarity. It may also mean probing your customers as to why they do what they do.

On one project, we had a reporting analyst who was adamant that a new system we were building produce an automated daily complex audit report on order and shipment activity that "management" needed. This person had been producing this report for a number of years and saw the report as crucial to running the business. We did some probing to find the report's customers, but unfortunately couldn't find any. It turns out that a manager who had since left the company had been using the report several years earlier. The report was literally being recycled each day without being looked at by anyone! A bit of probing never hurts....

If you're starting from a packaged application, consider the workflow of the new application and then try to fit your processes into the workflow. In some cases, due to your unique business requirements, there may be modifications needed to the application. At the same time, the application may actually do some things better than you do them today. Try to keep an open mind to adapting your processes to the application where you can.

There is a poor or non-existent design change process

You can be sure of one thing on a project: your first change request will plop itself on your doorstep within a few days after you freeze your design. Even with the best designs, business requirements change, things get missed, or items that were originally deemed out of scope become "must-have" requirements for the system. As much as you'd like to be able to ignore change requests, you can't if you want your project to succeed. After you freeze your design and start into development, a very deliberate change control process needs to be implemented.

The best change control processes that I have seen held the following things in common:

- Regular, deliberate meetings to review project change requests and determine disposition

- Agreed-upon criteria for accepting or rejecting change requests

- An escalation process for issues that needed to be brought to the executive sponsor or business owner for resolution

- A strong leader (typically the project manager) who is able to set agendas, drive decisions, and keep discussions constructive

The project manager should take clear ownership in establishing this process and getting the team gelled and harmonized as soon after design freeze as possible. Managing the change process is going to be difficult enough without having to deal with destructive attitudes, distrust, and hidden agendas. Even the best boards I've seen had some of these attributes, but the project manager was able to call it out and get things back on the constructive path quickly.

 **WARNING SIGNS**

There's no "voice of the customer" on the project

This may be stating the obvious, but if there is not adequate customer representation on your project, you've got major potential for your design not meeting customer need.

The project team customers can't see beyond how things are done today

If your customer team members are reluctant to changing from how they do things today to some better design, you're likely to include all the inefficiencies and outdated processes into your future design.

The customers are continually confused as to how they're going to do their job under the new design

When your customers are having a difficult time grasping how they are going to use the product you are designing, you are likely either not communicating clearly or have not incorporated the customer needs into the design. Either way, you risk customer rejection of your design.

The new design keeps changing late into the project

This is a really bad time for the customer to grasp how things are really going to work. Trying to figure out how a design will address a business problem during implementation is like trying to bait a fishing hook while under water.

The customers lose interest in the project and stop participating

So meetings come and go and your customers show up late, leave early, don't show up at all, or are not engaged while at the meeting. Emails don't get replies. Design decisions aren't being made. All signs that your customer doesn't believe in what you are doing and that you're losing (or have lost) their support. This warning sign could also manifest itself as customers being too busy doing their day-to-day job to participate on the project.

TURNING THINGS AROUND

Right-size customer involvement

Get customers with the right mindset and skill set involved in your project, and then make them owners of the solution. Make sure that they are able to look beyond how they do things today and can imagine a better world tomorrow with an improved product design. This could mean changing some of your customer project team members if they're not equipped to perform the job well.

Listen to the customer

If the customer is confused or skeptical of how the design will improve their lives, either their needs aren't being addressed properly or the design isn't being communicated well. Don't take anything for granted here; make sure that the customer knows how the product design is going to work and be prepared to adjust the design to ensure needs are met.

Slow down or stop the project to ensure that the design is going to meet business needs

As much as I don't like to do this, I have stopped projects and backtracked on product designs to make sure that what we were designing was addressing business needs. Stopping a project can be painful, and you'll probably take some near-term heat for doing so, but better you catch problems while still in development as opposed to your project being viewed as a failure because the solution didn't address the problem.

Keep true to your scope

In the heat of the moment (and your desire to please your customer) it can be very easy to forget about your original scope and start working on things that cause you to drift from your primary mission. Avoid distractions by deliberately keeping your scope at the forefront when making design decisions. Keep the project scope statement posted clearly where the project team can see it. At the same time, be prepared to do some scope adjusting if you see that you have missed something that is truly critical to the product design.

TAKE AWAYS

- Actively set scope on what the project will and won't focus on and get buy-in on the scope before starting the project

- Draw scope boundaries, but be prepared to redraw if business need dictates

- Involve a minimal number of dedicated customers very early in the design process

- Move deliberately through the design process with clear completion milestones

- Strongly consider using prototypes to flesh out your requirements and model any systems and process designs

- Make sure that you've wrung out bad processes or unverified assumptions prior to developing your product or solution

- Get your change control process put in place and get the team functioning effectively soon after the design is complete

We Used the
Wrong
Technology

When I was a consultant, I worked with for client who was implementing a shipping management system. The project had a lot of very good things happening. There was a very engaged and lively customer group. The sponsor was the CEO of the company and was actively engaged in the project. The project manager was very seasoned and had lots of experience implementing systems. There was only one little problem: they were implementing the system using a beta version of some of the key technology components that the entire system was reliant upon. This one little problem was enough to create a massive cost overrun, significantly delay implementation of the product, and burn out an entire team.

My intent in this chapter is not to outline different technologies or to advocate one technology over another. The technology choice is really specific to your environment and your specific business need. Having said that, there are some universal considerations for you to keep at the forefront when making your technology decision.

 # HOW IT HAPPENS

The technology is not time tested

Using new technologies can be very exciting for your project, particularly if the technology enables your customer to do things that they wouldn't be able to do otherwise. However, you should be very aware of the risks that you run with using technology that has not stood the test of time. When using a new technology, I would design into my project schedule specific go/no-go checkpoints based on extensive testing of the technology to better ensure that it was going to support the business need.

My preference on this is to not have to be the first to implement new or "bleeding edge" technology; I'd much rather learn from someone else when possible. When this isn't possible, though, it's helpful to give yourself some opportunities to stop the project before you get too far down the road and have a massive failure on your hands.

The technology does not meet the business functionality need

I've seen this happen a lot particularly with packaged application software. Someone at some point in time makes a decision to put in a software package without really understanding how the technology meets the business requirements. In particular, I've seen it happen when an assumption was made that business processes are similar regardless of the industry in which the process resides. For example, there are some fundamental differences in the procurement business process when comparing a defense manufacturer and a consumer goods company. In a defense manufacturer, parts are procured to a specific defense contract, have contract clauses that must be included in the purchase order for the contract, and can have different inspection criteria depending on the contract that the part is being procured against. A consumer goods company simply doesn't have to worry about the defense contract procurement process and wouldn't have the same degree of contract visibility to be concerned with.

One technique I've used quite effectively when implementing packaged application software is conducting scenario testing on the software using real-life business scenarios prior to designing any software or business process changes. As the software is tested, incompatibilities between the software and the business process are documented and tracked. Based on the issues identified, the project team makes a recommendation as to whether the software can be successfully used to support the business, where the software would need to be modified to fit the business, and where the business process would need to change to fit the software.

There are inexperienced people working with the technology

It very well could be that you've chosen outstanding technology that will meet the business needs, but if you don't have experienced people who understand the technology then your project is very likely to fail. If you are sold on using a particular technology but don't have the in-house expertise, you're far better off biting the cost bullet and bringing in consultants who not only know the technology but are able to help your developers get up to speed and be self-sustaining. Just make sure that the consultants you use truly have the experience needed or you're just paying to train them at the same time you're training your own team.

The technology isn't able to handle the volumes of the business

So the technology looks really good, the customers are happy with the functionality, and life looks grand. Then you implement it and the technology falls over because it can't handle the volumes. You then ask the question about volumes and find out that your 10,000 orders per week are about three times what the technology vendor's next largest customer does. A sad story indeed....

You want to make sure that the technology is industrial-strength enough to meet your current and anticipated business volumes. There are two effective ways to do this. First, get volumes from other customers who are running the solution to see if your volumes compare. Second, do a volume stress test on the technology in your environment to see how it performs. Both of these can be done very early in the design process and will give you a good early indication whether your technology will be able to meet the volume challenge.

WARNING SIGNS

The technology keeps failing during your project

If you continue to have problems with the technology performing its as-advertised functions throughout your project, this is probably a good warning that technology is going to continue to fail when your product is released to your customers.

You hear "it's in the next release" too much

When working with a third-party technology, be cautious about an overzealous vendor who promises quick fixes to problems or commits that features will be forthcoming in the next product release. It very well could be that your vendor is realistic about feature or fix deliveries, but it also could be that your vendor is committing first and figuring out how to deliver later.

Your customers keep complaining about the technology

The technology may be technically stable, but may simply not meet the business need. It's important to keep a tuned ear to your customer concerns. What you may interpret as resistance to change could actually be the technology not meeting the needs of your customer.

Your project team members who are responsible for the technology are taking longer than expected to fix problems

When technology problems seem to take longer than what you normally expect to fix, your project team members may not have the right experience or skill sets to address your problems and may actually be making things worse by inadvertently creating more problems in their attempt to fix things. While I'm a good project manager, I've learned the hard way that I should stay as far away as possible from anything having to do with furnaces or thermostats (as my local fire department will attest to).

TURNING IT AROUND

Test the technology until you're comfortable it's going to work

Build confidence that your technology is going to meet your customer need as early as you can in your project. As much as possible, make sure that your testing mirrors your real-life usage of the technology so that there is no question the technology will hold up to your customer demands. My view: better you test too much than not enough.

Get the right skills to work on and develop the technology

I've fired vendors, been fired as a vendor, and replaced project team members to make sure that people with the right skills were working on the technology. It's great to use your project to help educate others on the technology; just make sure that you've got enough people on the project who understand the technology and can teach more inexperienced team members.

Stop while it's still containable

If you see that the technology simply isn't going to work, stop work on the project that is dependent on the technology and assess your alternatives for other technologies. As undesirable as this may be, better you address the issue during the project than have your customer be impacted due to an inadequate technology.

 **TAKE AWAYS**

- Strive to implement technology that was time-tested; if that's not possible, do early testing to validate usability

- Make sure the technology meets the business need as defined by the customers

- Staff your project with team members experienced with the technology

- Ensure that the technology can handle current and future volumes that you're expecting

**We Didn't
Design a Good
Project
Schedule**

I can remember vividly my very first project schedule. My manager gave me the mission statement and an overall timeframe he thought it should take for me to complete the project. I diligently broke the schedule down to lower levels of detail. I continued to divide the overall timeframe among the tasks and assigned people to the tasks. I worked for days on end with my face buried in a computer screen developing the schedule. What I ended up with was a horrendously detailed project plan that had no logical dependencies identified, people being asked to complete 40-hour tasks in 15 minutes, and some people being asked to work 200 hours per week to get their work done. But by golly, the schedule met my manager's timeframe request.

Sadly enough (for me), this is a very true story but one that I don't think is too terribly uncommon. It's pretty easy to ignore reality at times when you're developing a schedule and to skip some fundamental steps in completing your schedule. You may get everything to look good on paper, but the result may deviate significantly from reality.

 # HOW IT HAPPENS

The project schedule is either too detailed or not detailed enough

A project schedule is only effective when it helps you know that everything is on track and that you're going to be able to complete the work on time. When your activities are at too high a level, you risk losing accountability, missing out on key dependencies or exposing yourself to "90% complete syndrome" when the team reports progress that is not real. When your activities are at too low a level, you can frustrate your team members by unduly micro-managing them, creating a greater administrative headache for yourself, and confusing the team with an excessive number of activities to manage. Either of these can spell schedule slippage and can severely impact successful project completion.

I've learned to use two rules of thumb when defining the appropriate level of detail for a project plan:

- Can the activity be assigned to a single person to complete the activity?

- Can the activity be completed in less than 40 hours?

Let me explain my question rationale. In the first question, I have found that explicit, clear lines of ownership are vital to ensuring that activities are completed. Whenever there is an activity assigned to "the team" or some other group of people there is no single point of accountability; thus, no one truly owns the task. Therefore, each and every task should have a named person that takes the heat if the task isn't completed on time.

In the second question, the more time an activity is given to complete, the greater the likelihood that you will be surprised at the last minute that the activity was not completed on time. I've gotten burned way too many times on an activity getting to 90% very quickly then taking twice the amount of time to finish the last 10%. Now, it's not that I'm a distrustful person or that I think that people are overtly trying to deceive me. No one wants to miss a deadline, so they will continue to report that they are on target and hope that everything falls into place if things start going awry. Sometimes it works; sometimes it doesn't. I prefer to leave as little to chance as possible. So, I've zeroed in on a 40-hour rule of thumb because it allows you to break activities into manageable chunks and gives more frequent deadlines so you know sooner if the project is off track. In addition, the rule gives the team member a bit of breathing room and avoids them feeling micromanaged. Depending on your environment, you may want to use something other than 40 hours, just be definitive and consistent in what you use.

The project schedule doesn't correctly address dependencies between tasks

When designing your project schedule, keep in mind how those activities relate to other activities and define them accordingly. Establishing clear dependencies between tasks and having a true understanding of the critical path (the string of tasks that are the longest point between the start and finish of the project) is, in my view, one of the most important components of your project schedule. As you're designing your schedule activities, it's helpful to keep dependencies clean by defining clear finish-to-start relationships. There are ways to accommodate this by using most common project management software packages, but I recommend keeping your dependencies simple to understand and manage.

The project duration is too long

When designing your schedule, keep specific focus on the length of time that you go between celebrating successes. I've become a strong advocate of keeping project phases to no longer than three months in duration. This is not to say that if you are implementing an Enterprise Resource Planning system you should try to do the entire implementation from software selection to implemented system in that three-month timeframe. What I am saying is that you should phase the project in such a way that there is a defined beginning and end to the phase within three months. Why would I say such a thing? Simple: people (particularly managers) live in a short attention span theatre world and over time will become discouraged and lose interest if a project drags on too long. OK, you've figured me out—I'm just breaking a $10 bill into two $5 bills. Frequently, I've seen teams perform better when they are able to have mini celebrations at the successful end of each phase because at any point in time the end of the phase of work is no more than three months away. This also gives the team and management logical review points to look at the project's mission and ensure that it is in sync with management's current priorities.

Some of the tasks don't produce useful deliverables

When you're defining your project schedule, make sure you're continually asking yourself these questions:

- What is the deliverable that will be produced out of this activity?
- What will it look like?
- What happens if we don't do it?

If you don't have satisfactory answers to each of these questions, seriously consider whether or not the activity is necessary. Remember every activity that should get you one step closer to successful completion. If you can't articulate what the activity is supposed to produce, chances are that you don't need to do it.

The team doesn't understand the plan

Your project team needs to have complete buy-in on the tasks, duration, team assignments, dependencies, and deliverables. What I've seen work well is doing shorter, more frequent informal reviews with team members while you're developing the schedule. I've seen project managers hole themselves up in an office or conference room for days on end, emerge from their cave with the "schedule to end all schedules," and then have the other team members storm the Bastille because they don't see how they're possibly going to be able to accomplish what the project manager expects (recall my opening story about my unrealistic schedule). On days like those, the project manager wonders why he or she didn't take over the family delicatessen instead of doing this stupid project manager job. Get the buy-in along the way; it helps you avoid rework, allows the team members to feel more included in the process, and produces a better quality plan that the team will believe they can achieve.

WARNING SIGNS

Tasks aren't getting done on time

Chronically missed deadlines on tasks can be due to unrealistic task duration, poorly defined dependencies, poorly defined work assignments, or project distractions. Diagnose the reasons for the missed deadlines immediately before the snowball rolling down the hill turns into an avalanche.

Tasks assigned to "the team" or some other group of people aren't getting done

Any time that a specific name is not attached to a task, it is easy for team members to assume that someone else will do the task because *no one is specifically held accountable for task completion.* If you want things to get done, make sure that there are specific names beside each of your task and that each team member feels personal accountability for getting their work done.

Team members aren't aware that they are supposed to be working on a task

It's an ugly situation when you're getting status updates from team members and a task that was supposed to be completed last week wasn't even started because the team member didn't even know they were supposed to be working on the task. Make sure that work assignments are crystal clear and that team members know what tasks they are supposed to have completed by when.

Team members are confused as to what they are supposed to produce for a task

So you assign a task to a team member and the day that the task is due the team member produces a deliverable that looks exactly *nothing* like you were expecting it to look like. The deliverable now needs to be reworked which means other tasks are going to slip as a result. Be clear about what deliverable needs to be produced and ensure that you and the team member have a common understanding of what it needs to look like.

TURNING IT AROUND

Get real with the schedule, and fast

Don't delay; get the schedule in shape quickly, making sure that you've defined all the right tasks, duration, dependencies, and resources to get it done. More importantly, don't go into a cave for days on end to do it; make sure that you are getting input on the schedule frequently to avoid an unrealistic schedule.

Do focused reviews with team members

On some projects, I have developed supplemental documentation which explains key tasks that might be confusing, and have even gone so far as to produce a template of what the deliverable out of the task needed to look like. I prefer to do mini reviews as the plan is being developed to ensure that the team is putting their thumbprint on the plan and that any confusion points can be addressed early.

Keep dependencies simple

While it's great to clearly understand dependencies between tasks, I've also seen plans that are overly complicated because the project manager built in serial dependencies between tasks that could actually be performed in parallel. This could be due to an assumed dependency between the tasks or because the project manager is anticipating that one person will be doing both tasks. Before defining a dependency, put rigor into making sure that the tasks are truly reliant on being performed serially.

Highlight tasks that are due in the next 1-2 weeks

I've learned through experience that solely relying on the project schedule as the communication vehicle for a project team is not always the most effective way of ensuring that tasks get done on time. Depending on the experience of your team, they may not understand how to read the schedule and may miss some key tasks that need to get done. I've learned to use either status reports or e-mail reminders to individual team members reminding them of what they need to do and when it needs to be done. It puts a bit more work on the project manager, but it better ensures that the team member knows what needs to be done by when.

 **TAKE AWAYS**

- Make sure that all your lowest level activities have a sole owner and are no longer than 40 hours in duration.

- Break your project into phases that don't exceed three schedule months.

- Know the critical path of tasks through the project and keep clean finish-to-start dependencies between activities.

- Make sure that your activities have associated deliverables that are relevant.

- Ensure that the team buys into the plan along the way; don't do a grand reveal when the plan is complete.

- Remind and highlight team members regarding tasks that need to be completed within 1-2 weeks.

Screw-up
#5

We Didn't Have
the Right
Sponsorship

Some years back I was appointed the lead program manager on an initiative which had as its objective to consolidate a number of disparate order management systems into a single system which supported all of the company's order management needs. There were about five program managers working with me who each dragged in their respective customers to participate in the project. The project was sponsored by the IT organization with no sponsorship from the business owner. The project lumbered along for about two months with the customers continually questioning why they were working on a project that wasn't on their manager's radar. The business owner finally had enough and called IT management and the lead program manager (me!) into a meeting. The meeting started off with the manager saying to IT, "Who told you to go do this project?" Now, I'm no rocket scientist, but it was pretty clear at that point that this was not to be one of my shining project management moments. While the meeting was very uncomfortable, I learned an extremely important lesson: absolutely, without a doubt, secure sponsorship on a project at the beginning, or suffer the consequences.

For any project, it's crucial to get an appropriate level of project sponsorship. The ideal project sponsor for your project would possess the following characteristics:

- He/she directly experiences the pain of the status quo and would directly benefit as a result of doing the project
- He/she actively helped craft the project mission statement
- He/she has the decision making authority to secure or re-allocate resources to/from other projects as necessary to ensure that your project can be completed successfully
- He/she is willing to go to bat for your project with peer managers if you need help in getting something from another organization
- He/she is willing to meet with you on a regular basis to ensure that you're getting what you need to succeed

- He/she is willing to make difficult decisions that may be unpopular but are in the best interests of the business
- He/she has some "skin in the game" to ensure the project's success

Now, I recognize that as a project manager you only have so much control over your project sponsor. Nonetheless, it's important to diligently try to manage your project sponsor to ensure that you're getting what you need from him/her.

Depending on the scope of your project, it may be beneficial to have a steering committee in place in addition to the project sponsor. Your steering committee is typically comprised of key managers of your stakeholder organizations. The primary functions of a steering committee involve

- Being a decision-making body on key issues that cannot be resolved by the project team
- Eliminating any project barriers that the project team is running up against
- Being a supporter of any resultant change that the project will bring about to their respective organizations
- Providing counsel and guidance to the project team on key aspects of the design and implementation of the product
- Assisting the project manager in securing required resources for the project
- Providing recommendations to the project sponsor on major issues which are beyond the authority of the steering committee

You need to decide whether a steering committee is beneficial to the project. Some criteria that I have used on projects are as follows:

- There are multiple stakeholders that are directly affected by the outcome of the project
- There are internal or external subject matter experts that can provide functional, technical, or execution guidance to the project team

- The project sponsor has limited time to spend on the project and delegates some of the project decision-making responsibility to the steering committee

I've successfully completed projects with and without a steering committee depending on the criteria mentioned, but every successful project *always* had an engaged project sponsor.

HOW IT HAPPENS

The project sponsor is either too high or too low in the organization

Just because you have someone who is willing to sponsor your project doesn't mean that they are the *right* sponsor for the project. Optimally, your project sponsor should have decision-making authority over the in-scope project areas while at the same time being close enough to the work that they understand the implications of the issues that are raised. If your sponsor is too low-level, they're unlikely to be able to make decisions that will stick and will have to be getting authorization from their management before committing to decisions. If your sponsor is too high-level, you're likely to get decisions made but you're probably not making best use of management because others at lower levels could be making the decisions you need made.

The project sponsor is being inundated with issues that could be resolved by a steering committee

In deciding whether or not you need a steering committee, consider what you're going to need from your project sponsor and whether or not decisions can be made by others at lower management levels. If you are continually bringing issues to your project sponsor that can be addressed by other managers, you run the risk of exasperating your sponsor and being labeled as crying wolf. This will put you in a very difficult situation for when you really need help because your credibility with your project sponsor may be eroded.

You make the project sponsor work too hard to try to understand your project

In the environments that I have worked, I never gave a project sponsor anything other than presentation-type slides when it came to project reviews and requests for help. Typically, your time with the project sponsor is limited and he or she has to understand where things are and what you need from him or her in an efficient manner. Be very conscious of what you share with the sponsor, how much detail you give him/her, and what you want him/her to do for you to help the project succeed.

You walk a fine line here of being credible with your sponsor and giving them the elevator pitch. If you've already established credibility with your project sponsor to the point where you're a trusted project manager, then you can possibly afford to be more high level in your communications because he or she is going to trust you with the details. If you're an unknown quantity or (gulp) have gone negative in the credibility column, you're going to need to be prepared for deep-dives on areas that the project sponsor will want to go. One technique I've seen and used is to have appendix slides which have supporting detail in areas where there's likely to be question. The appendix slides are only meant to be used in the event that a specific question arises to support your claims and would not even be seen if no question arises on the topic.

Being prepared to go through details is important, but there will be the occasional situation where you just don't know the answer or don't have supporting detail. Your best bet at that point is to simply say, "I don't know, and I'll get back to you on <put date here> with the answer." It's much easier to fess up quickly than guess at the answer and later be found wrong. Keep in mind as well that there are only so many "I don't knows" you can use before your credibility becomes an issue. More than a couple in a meeting can turn into a problem pretty quickly.

You don't tell the project sponsor what you need

Working with a project sponsor is a two-way commitment; you need to deliver what the sponsor considers to be important and they need to help you when you've run into an issue you can't resolve on your own. The issue could be with another organization, a need to change policy, a team member not participating as agreed, or a host of other reasons. It's super-important that you are very explicit with what you need the project sponsor to do for you. In your reviews with the project sponsor, it's helpful to have an "asks" slide that very explicitly lays out what you need the project sponsor to do and when you need it by. As I've discussed earlier, make sure that your requests are appropriate for your project sponsor to be addressing. If your requests are inappropriate, you run the risk of exasperating your project sponsor and losing credibility.

You meet either too much or not enough with your project sponsor

Depending on the criticality of the project, you may need to meet with the project sponsor either more or less frequently. I've been on projects where we've met with the project sponsor on a monthly basis for a one-hour update and have also been on projects where we've met weekly for an hour or more. You need to decide along with your project sponsor what the right frequency needs to be. I've found that meeting at least monthly is important to keeping the sponsor engaged and ensuring project success.

 # WARNING SIGNS

You don't have an identified project sponsor

If you're running a project and don't have someone at an appropriate level in the organization sponsoring the work, then you most likely don't have a viable, sanctioned project, and it's just a matter of time before the project meets an abrupt end. Someone at an appropriate level in the company needs to care enough about the work that you're doing to sponsor it. If not, then you're better off stopping the work yourself before someone stops it for you.

You can't get the project sponsor's attention

Cancelled meetings, unresponsive emails, and unreturned calls are all signs that your project sponsor isn't engaged, doesn't care, is the wrong person, or has more important things to do. Regardless of the reason, if your sponsor won't give you the time of day then you're unlikely to get the support for your project when you really need it.

Your project sponsor doesn't help you with management issues

Your project sponsor has a responsibility to the project to provide guidance on key issues that materially impact the resulting work product. When armed with the right decision factors, a good project sponsor provides direction on key issues in a timely manner and keeps the project moving forward. I've seen some project sponsors, though, that are either unwilling or unable to provide direction on key issues which can ultimately stall out a project. Having an unwilling or indecisive project sponsor is a pretty clear signal that you've got the wrong sponsorship for the project.

TURNING THINGS AROUND

Make sure that your project sponsor is current and engaged

Do a regular status meeting with your project sponsor and make sure that they know the status of the project, where there are problems, and what you need from them to keep the project moving forward. Make sure that they know enough about the project so that when you need them to make decisions you're not spending unnecessary time getting them up to speed on project basics.

Clarify your project sponsor's expectations

Identify the expectations of your project sponsor at the onset of the project to ensure that you're working towards a common end result and that project deliverables are in line with what your sponsor wants. Periodically validate the expectations to ensure that any changes in expectations are clearly communicated and understood between you and the project sponsor.

Right-size your time with your project sponsor

Chances are, your project sponsor has a long to-do list of things and does not want to feel like his or her time is being wasted. Determine with your sponsor the frequency, time and method of communications that you need and **stick to it**.

Tell your project sponsor explicitly what you need for the project to succeed

As discussed earlier, let your project sponsor know what you need him or her to do to ensure project success. Be as explicit as possible. But, make sure your requests are appropriate. Don't ask your sponsor to make decisions that others (or you) could be making.

Strongly consider stopping the project

If you aren't able to secure appropriate sponsor engagement, you should think strongly about stopping the project and refocusing resources on other projects that management cares about.

 **TAKE AWAYS**

- Make sure that your project sponsor is interested, engaged, and active in the project
- Actively decide if a steering committee is necessary for the project in addition to having the project sponsor
- Raise issues to the project sponsor that are appropriate for him or her to resolve
- Keep your communication very clear, crisp, and credible
- Be very clear about what you need the project sponsor to do to ensure project success
- Deliberately decide with the project sponsor how frequently you need to meet based on the criticality of the project

The Team
Didn't Gel

I played the drums as a kid starting in fourth grade up into college. My family suffered through many hours (and headaches) of me beating the skins to jazz, funk, and rock music. When I started playing with the school band, I had to learn that making music wasn't about how fast I could do flam-a-diddles or how loud I could play, but how I played in relation to the other band members. If the music called for *adagio* (slow & leisurely pace) it would be a bad idea to break into an "In-A-Gadda-Da-Vida" drum solo while everyone else is playing elevator music. The important thing was to match my playing to the other instrumentalists and to make beautiful music together. While I never got to rock stardom with my own entourage and groupies, I did learn that music is about how the entire band sounds — not any individual player.

By now you're probably wondering why I took a mental trip to Tahiti to tell you about my musical aspirations. To me, a well-structured project team where each team member understands their role in making the project successful is like the musicians playing in a band. Each project team member knows what they need to contribute to the project, when they have to perform, what other project team members are doing on the project, and what it takes to be successful. Just as important, each of the project team members helps each other to ensure overall project success.

 **HOW IT HAPPENS**

There is not a clear project organization with clearly defined roles

This goes beyond a hierarchy chart. Each person needs to know what function they play on the team, how they fit into the other functions, and what happens if they don't do their job.

Depending on your industry or functional discipline, there may be standard or customary roles that you employ on your project. There are a few things that I have learned, though, about project standard roles as follows:

- Start with the standard or customary roles that are typical for your type of projects
- If the project need warrants a special role which is outside of standard, create a special role
- If the project doesn't need a standard or customary role, eliminate the role

These may sound like overly simplistic statements, but I've been amazed over the years with seeing cumbersome project role structures because the project manager was reluctant to deviate from standard project roles. As experienced project managers, our job first and foremost is to make sure that the right people are assigned to do the right tasks to produce the right result at the right time. At the end of the day, I've never been graded on how well I adhered to a standard project role structure; I've been graded on results.

If the project environment doesn't have standard or customary project roles or if I'm taking on a unique type of project, I like to take a very pragmatic approach to role definition, as follows:

- Define the 3-6 things on the project that I am most concerned about or pose the greatest risk to me
- Create roles that encompass the concern or risk areas
- Cross-check the roles with the work that needs to be done in the project schedule to ensure that all the major roles are being defined correctly

By doing this, I am addressing concern or risk areas head-on by defining a role with a singular point of accountability to manage the areas of my project that are most likely to fail. This technique has helped me on more than one project to sleep better knowing that I had my most crucial areas covered.

The team finger points and fights in public

On any project you do, so long as there is more than one person involved, there are going to be lively discussions. When this happens, it is very likely that something good will come of the discussion and that in some way the project will move one step closer to the finish line as a result. On past projects I have managed, I was very deliberate about letting these discussions happen and in letting team members question each other. I did put a few rules in place, though:

- It's very cool to challenge and stretch, but when we make a decision we need to get behind it as a team
- What happens in the room stays in the room; outside of the room we are a unified team
- If we made a wrong decision we accept the decision as a team; no finger pointing allowed
- We focus on the problem and not the person; don't make the problem personal

So, were the rules followed 100% of the time? Sadly, no (myself included). After all, we are human. However, you should still strive to get some ground rules in place to avoid team strife where you can.

There is no "rallying cry"

You can look at many major successful campaigns and pull some slogans from them which embodied the message behind the slogan: "Where's the beef," "Milk, it does a body good," and "Plop, plop, fizz, fizz" are all unifying messages that cause you to think about a product. Similarly, when driving a project it helps the team to have some kind of a rallying cry or mantra that the team embodies when driving work. On one project, we wanted to be extremely cautious of not over-designing a solution and putting too many bells and whistles in to help us keep our costs down. We started using a "good enough" rallying cry during the design phase to be a continual reminder that we wanted to not overdo the solution. It worked incredibly well because the team would critically question itself with "Is this good enough?" when looking at the architecture and functionality. Aside from helping to make sure that our solution was cost effective, the rallying cry helped the team to better bond.

Team members aren't held accountable for delivery

With project teams, I firmly believe that each role needs to clearly understand what they need to do, when they need it done by, and how their work fits into the big picture. I also firmly believe the project team isn't only accountable to the project manager, they are accountable to each other because if any of the other roles fail the entire team fails. Given so, it is vitally important for each role to be visible as to what each other role is doing for the following reasons:

- Each role should be continually looking at other work that is happening to ensure that they know if and how they fit into the other work
- Each role should feel that if they miss a deadline or do not perform their job adequately, they are letting down the team as a whole, not just the project manager.
- Meeting or missing deadlines and deliverables are a team issue and should be exposed to the team.

The point here is accountability. Each member needs to feel accountable for his or her work and needs to experience the joy of success as well as the discomfort of failure. The project manager needs to use discretion on making sure that things do stay constructive. Focus should be very much on how the team gets things back on track and moving forward versus badgering the team member.

In some instances, though, you may just have someone in a job who is not suited to perform. The project manager needs to deal with those situations swiftly because if he or she doesn't, he or she is not doing his job nor being accountable to the team by dealing with a problem performer.

The project manager isn't suited for the job

The project's needs and criticality to the business will be key drivers in the required experience level of the project manager. For relatively simple projects, you may be able to staff the project with an inexperienced project manager with a more seasoned project manager serving as an occasional mentor. As projects increase in complexity and criticality to the business, though, there's no substitute for an experienced, seasoned project manager.

I've been incredibly fortunate to have worked with some outstanding project managers over the years. In thinking about the best project managers, they've had the following things in common:

- They knew the techniques of project management cold
- They knew (through experience) where they could bend the rules on the techniques to be able to buy time or be more efficient
- They always kept things moving forward
- They knew when to shift from "let's discuss" mode to "let's decide" mode
- They held others accountable to do their jobs
- They praised success
- They were excellent communicators
- They took the heat for the team when external criticism happened
- They were calm and focused when things started going bad on a project and everyone else was wigging out

I know of no magic formula for fitting the project manager for the job; what I can say is you're better to err on having an over-experienced project manager versus an under-experienced one.

I knew of a very gung-ho young project manager (let's just call him "Author") who felt he was an outstanding project manager because he knew the techniques well (cost and schedule management, status reporting, and so on). Because Author knew the techniques, he felt he could simultaneously take on three complex projects that really should have each had a dedicated project manager. Not only did Author learn some very valuable lessons, he unfortunately also cost his company a lot of money because others had to come in and mop up his mess. Both Author and I can't stress enough to make sure your project manager is suited for the job.

The team doesn't celebrate wins

Driving through a project is tough work. It is incredibly easy for people to get discouraged whenever the team hits roadblocks or has setbacks. It is vitally important for a team to celebrate hitting key milestones simply to keep morale up and keep project momentum. I'm not talking about three-day cruise type celebrations, it could be as simple as bringing in pizza or cake or something that allows people to let their hair down and take a bit of a breather. I would caution you about doing this too much; doing too much celebration lessens the effect of the celebration and could actually annoy your team members. I was on one project where people did not like the morale events because it only meant that they had to stay later that evening to get their work done. So, celebrate, but do it in moderation.

 **WARNING SIGNS**

The team shows confusion about who is doing what

Confusion can exist either due to poor communication on who is responsible for what tasks or because tasks can fit within the context of more than one role. It's important not only to get people to agree on areas of responsibility, but to ensure that the responsibilities are clearly documented and communicated to the entire project team. Also, be prepared to pull this document out and remind the team of its respective responsibilities as confusion creeps back into the project team.

Discussions are destructive and unproductive

You know what this looks like; if you're team can't have discussions without getting personal, derogatory, or outright mean this is a pretty clear sign you're not gelling as a team. The project team doesn't have to be best friends with each other, but they should at least respect what each other bring to the table.

Team members aren't helping each other

I've actually been in some environments as a consultant where some team members enjoyed seeing other team members fail and did absolutely nothing to help them for the good of the project. Project team members who carry an "every person for themselves" kind of attitude are not going to perform anywhere near their full potential.

 **TURNING IT AROUND**

Clarify the confusion

Get team members locked in a room and hammer this out. If you get stuck on a particularly contentious area or if you see tempers flaring, set it aside and work on other things, then come back to the contentious area. Make sure that responsibilities are documented and clearly accessible for all members.

Address the problem team member

Never a pleasant task, but on more than one occasion I have had a project team member taken off the project because they simply were going to remain a destructive force on the project. At the same time, I've also been able to turn a destructive situation around. In either event, address the issue swiftly before it does further damage to the rest of the project team.

Co-locate the team

I've had some of my greatest successes where the project team was physically located in the same area and had minimal physical barriers to inhibit communication. This may or may not be entirely possible depending on your project, but where you have the opportunity to co-locate team members, strongly consider doing so.

Go out for a milkshake

Sometimes it's great to just get people away from their work environment and socialize over a favorite food and beverage. As a consultant on out-of-town projects, our project teams were typically very effective because we had more time to socialize and bond during non-work hours. Getting to know each other a bit and being able to laugh as a team pays huge dividends in overall team effectiveness.

All work and no play...

...makes for a really dull and demotivating project. Take some time out of the project to have a laugh. I have certainly been known to play an occasional practical joke on a project or to bring some occasional levity to a particularly stressful time in a project. Just be careful that the use of humor isn't too excessive or inappropriate; but by all means make sure that you share a laugh or two even if it's at your expense.

Be the unifier

As the project manager, you are expected to take responsibility for getting the team to gel and to know the barriers that exist which are preventing the team from being a highly cohesive, collaborative, high-performance team. At times, it's likely to be the most uncomfortable part of your job, but it can also be one of the most rewarding when done well.

 **TAKE AWAYS**

- Define a clear project organization with clearly defined roles
- Be a team through thick and thin; don't publicly finger-point when things start going south
- Develop a "rallying cry" which focuses the team on the mission
- Let the team members do their jobs, but hold them accountable for results and dates
- Make sure that you have a project manager that who is appropriately seasoned for the project
- Celebrate the wins as a team

We Didn't
Involve the
Right People

Some years back I worked on a process re-engineering project at a large industrial manufacturer. The project went on for several months and it looked as if things were going quite well. Then, a person that I'll call "Hack" showed up on the project who reported to one of the divisional VPs. Hack came into the project with a negative viewpoint, and after a couple of weeks was successful in convincing the divisional VP that the project should be shut down. The project team packed up and was out of there that day. In looking at the situation, had we involved Hack earlier in the project we could have made some fundamental changes in the direction which would have put the project on a path more in line with management expectations and avoided wasting time and money on the project.

Chances are, there has been a Hack on one of your projects who showed up, disrupted everything and either slowed down or derailed your project completely. It could be that it was the wrong business decision to shut the project down, but it could also be that it was the *right* thing to do because the project wasn't addressing the collective need of the customer. Regardless of right or wrong, it is very important to know whom to involve in your project to better ensure success and avoid the waste and frustration of a stalled project.

So, let's talk about the people, or *stakeholders,* who aren't assigned to the project but can materially influence its outcome. In my experience, stakeholders generally fall into two groups: customer stakeholders, or those you help, and supplier stakeholders, or those who help you. Your customer stakeholders primarily are going to be your customer population along with their associated management. At the end of the day, they are going to be the ultimate judge of your end product and will be your ultimate measure of success. Your supplier stakeholders can be quite varied. Technical support personnel, consultants, and third-party software providers are all examples of supplier stakeholders. As you design your project, you'll need to think about the type of help that you will need and enlist support from your supplier stakeholders to help ensure success.

HOW IT HAPPENS

There is not clear definition on who the customer is

Getting your customer list right and making them aware of the project early on is super important in avoiding project stalls and fire drills that occur because someone is bent out of shape that they weren't included. Something that I've learned (again, the hard way) is that you very well could be doing everything right on your project and that the project is being done for all the right reasons. However, if someone was not included (but should have been) in the project at the beginning and "finds out" that the project is going on, you have a situation on your hands. You not only need to orient them to the project and get their commitment, but also smooth ruffled feathers because you didn't include them in the first place. Many times things work out OK, but you've taken time away from other activities to deal with a fire drill that could have been avoided had you better defined the customer list at project onset.

Others who could help with specific issues on the project aren't utilized

On one project for which I was the business owner, an employee relatively new to the company was working to aggregate worldwide financial planning information and report it to senior finance management. He did an outstanding job of defining the information requirements, setting up the reporting infrastructure, and managing the team members assigned to him to complete the project. He came up against a project issue and was working hours on end trying to get the issue resolved among the project team. When he raised the issue to me, I asked him if he had contacted the group in the company that had expertise on the very issue he was trying to solve on his own. The end of the story is that he solicited help from the group and they resolved the issue that afternoon. Knowing who can help you get through tough project issues can save you tons of time and frustration and avoid wasting precious project resources.

The people who can torpedo a project aren't identified and managed

Just as in my "Hack" example above, it will help you immensely to know who is likely to create trouble for your project. When I was a consultant doing a project in a particularly political or contentious environment, we would review the customer's organization chart with the customer project manager and identify friends and foes of the project. With project friends, we maintained the relationship with them by keeping them briefed on project progress to ensure that they remained friends. With the foes, we took deliberate steps to meet with them, review the project with them, understand their reservations, and attempt to let them put their thumbprint on the project to make it more palatable to them. Sometimes this was successful where a foe became a friend of the project, but other times the foe remained a foe and we had to rely on the project sponsor to help us manage the foe. Either way, know who can hurt you and actively manage the relationship with them.

 **WARNING SIGNS**

You're getting a lot of questions from other stakeholder groups on what you're doing

Sometimes this could simply be that stakeholder groups are curious about your project and find it interesting. This could also mean, though, that there are stakeholders that should have a voice in your project and are currently not being heard. Be aware of assessing the degree of involvement that other stakeholder group needs to have on your project and be open to involving them based on business need.

Uninvited stakeholders start showing up at project meetings

So you're in a project status meeting and a stakeholder that has previously not been associated with the project shows up. It very well could be that the stakeholder has a need to know what's going on and they just need to get up to speed on the project. It may be the right thing to involve the stakeholder, but avoid allowing the stakeholder to hijack your meeting and waste other participants' time by getting a project briefing during a time where other project business was slated to be discussed.

Project issues are taking longer than expected to resolve

If team members appear to be spinning their wheels on a project issue, it could be that they are not involving the right subject matter experts and are attempting to wrestle the issue to the ground on their own. Take the time to work with them to make sure that resources available to them are being utilized appropriately.

TURNING IT AROUND

Communicate, communicate, communicate

I've always found that, unless there are specific confidentiality constraints that forbid you from discussing the project outside of a small group, communication on what you're doing to different stakeholder groups is crucial. Have a standard pitch that you can give at a moment's notice to a group of people that describes the project.

Know whom to call

As I mentioned previously, don't slog through issues on your own if you don't have to. Whenever I run up against a difficult issue on a project, my first thought is "Who can help me resolve this?"

Be continually seeking out subject matter experts to help get you through problems. It not only makes your life easier, it better ensures a more successful project completion.

Right-size project involvement

Just because someone wants to be involved in a project (or shows up as an uninvited stakeholder) doesn't necessarily mean that there is a business need for them to be involved. You've got to make conscious decisions on who is involved in a project and to what degree they are involved. Their involvement could be as an interested party that gets a briefing on some periodic basis. Then again, their involvement could be as a decision-maker because the product you are producing will have a direct impact on their business.

Let your project sponsor help you

When defining your stakeholders, use your project sponsor to help you with the identification. They will likely know the organization better than you and can help ensure that the right people get involved in the project. You may also need your project sponsor to help you with a foe that is creating problems for you.

Be open to adjusting the focus and scope of the project

If it turns out that you didn't include the right stakeholders at project onset, be open to refining your focus and scope to ensure that your project is addressing your true stakeholder needs. Use your project sponsor to help you in this refinement and in working with the other stakeholders to decide on how business needs either are or aren't met.

TAKE AWAYS

- Know who your customer is and involve them up front
- Know who can help you get things done; don't try to do everything yourself
- Know who can torpedo your project and manage the relationship with them

Screw-up #8

We Didn't Communicate What We Were Doing

Television commercials. Thirty very structured seconds which follow the time-tested AIDA (Attention, Interest, Desire, and Action) marketing principle. As irritating as some commercials may be, commercials are effective in promoting awareness about a product or service and are a proven method of getting you to buy what the advertiser is selling.

So what do commercials have to do with how you communicate your project? A good communication plan is very similar to a good commercial in the following ways:

- The communication is targeted to a specific audience
- The communication gets your attention
- The communication is embedded into something that the audience is already engaged in
- The communication is brief but relevant and informative
- The communication clearly states what you as the audience need to do if you want whatever is being advertised

Putting together and executing a solid communications plan with your audience is going to be a crucial aspect of ensuring that your project is ultimately successful. Let's drill into what makes a communication plan effective.

There will be a number of groups that will somehow be influenced by the result of your project. In prior chapters I talked about the project team, executive sponsor, steering committee, and stakeholder groups. These are all audiences that should be included in your communications plan. In addition, you may have some other interested parties that may not directly be impacted by your project but may have some indirect interest. For example, if you are doing project that is deploying a new technology, there may be other groups in your organization that would have an interest in the technology and in learning from you. The important thing here is to clearly define your specific audiences you want to communicate with.

After you've defined your audiences, you need to think about what each specific audience is going to need from you, how frequently they're going to need it, and how they're going to get it.

The very best communication plans that I have seen all start with a one-page communications matrix. This matrix clearly spells out the following for each audience:

- The audience
- Type of communication the audience is going to receive
- Purpose of the communication
- Owner of the communication
- Frequency that the audience will receive it
- The medium (email, presentation, and so on) in which the communication will be delivered

For example, see the following table:

Communication type	Purpose	Owner	Frequency	Medium	Project Team	Customers	Supplier Stake-holders	Steering Committee	Executive Management
							Audiences		
Status Reports	Provide detailed status on project progress.	Project Manager	Weekly	Email	X	X	X	X	
Project Briefings	Provide overview of project purpose, deliverables and timeframe	Customer Project Team Member	Once at beginning of project	Live presentation at staff meetings		X	X	X	X
Status Meetings	Discuss project schedule, risks, issues and costs.	Project Manager	Weekly	Live meeting	X				
Executive memo	Memo which outlines why project is being done and importance of project to organization.	Project Sponsor	Once at beginning of project	Email	X	X	X	X	X

In designing your communications matrix, you can either have audiences down the side or the communication types, as long as your matrix is easy to understand.

Next, let's talk about content of the communication. The best project communications that I've seen share the following characteristics:

- It uses as few words as possible to get the point across
- It is tailored for the specific audience to only give them what they need
- It uses a medium that the makes the audience most likely to look at the communication
- It clearly spells out what actions the audience needs to take, if any

Your communication should also blend into the culture so that reading your communication is embedded into the audience's typical workflow. In my email-intensive culture, virtually all of my communication is done via email. Routing things hard-copy simply isn't done and would very quickly cast a negative shadow on the project. In addition, rather than sending attachments in the email, I will try to copy and paste relevant content right into the body of the email. My experience is that the audience is more likely to read and respond to an email when the information is embedded in the body versus the recipient having to open up another document. This can't always be done, particularly if the document is large, but consider doing it where possible. You may also consider using real-time venues (such as town hall meetings, "brown bag" lunch meetings, staff briefings, and so on) to get your words across. The important thing is to fit your communication to your culture.

Lastly, the communication very explicitly outlines what action the audience is expected to take and when it needs to be taken by. The best communications that I've seen on this always have a "What do you need to do" section, even if there is no specific action required by the audience. It provides very explicit guidance to the audience as to what you expect from them and when, and forces you to keep your communication tight and relevant.

HOW IT HAPPENS

Audiences are not defined clearly

At the beginning of your project, take the time to clearly think through who your audience groups are and why they need to be included in your project communications. Make sure that you are getting feedback on your audience group definitions and that the project team, steering committee, and project sponsor agrees with the definitions.

You create a great communication plan but it isn't followed

As the project manager, it's your responsibility to make sure that communications happen when the plan says they're going to happen and the audiences get the communication that they're expecting. I've seen plans fall apart, particularly if things start going bad on a project. It's at times like this that very relevant, concise, and deliberate communication is most important on the project. If you as the project manager "go silent" on a project, your audience groups are left with tapping into the rumor mill on what's happening on the project. Rumor mills are rarely flattering and could mean that you will end up spending more time fielding one-off requests by concerned stakeholders than you would if you had taken the deliberate communications route.

The communication isn't tuned to the audience

Make sure that you are taking into account what communication is being sent to whom and that it is concise, relevant, and timely for them. Don't be lazy on this and try to take a "one size fits all" with your communication; your end result is likely to frustrate your audiences and leave your communications unread.

I once worked on a project where the project manager sent virtually every document the project created to all his audience groups. The rationale that the project manager used was that he wanted to be "very open" with the project and wanted all audience groups to have complete access to any information about the project. While being very open about a project is a good thing, what ended up happening was that the audiences got incredibly frustrated with the sheer amount of information they were receiving and ended up ignoring anything that this project manager sent out. So, the communication plan of "send everything to everyone" ended up being a fatal error in the project's success

The communication doesn't come from the right person

You could be communicating all the right things, but if it isn't coming from the right person on the project your communication is less likely to be received as intended. For instance, if you are trying to garner support for the project, having the project sponsor deliver the communication would be more effective than the project manager delivering the communication. Similarly, project status reports shouldn't come from a lower-level project team member; they should come from the project manager.

 **WARNING SIGNS**

Your audience asks questions about the project that you've already communicated

Whenever I've gotten these types of questions I've learned to take my hands off the keyboard to avoid typing a terse "Didn't you read my status report" type of response. It very well could be that they aren't paying attention to your standard communications, or it could be that they're unable to understand your communication.

You're getting a lot of one-off requests for project information from audiences not in your communication plan

When audiences that are not included in your standard communications are repeatedly asking for information, this could be a sign that you don't have all the right audiences identified for communication; if they are already in the plan, it could be that your communication to them isn't frequent enough.

Your audience requests go unanswered

So you send out a communication asking for something from your audience and you get very little response. It could be that your audience isn't reading your communication, or it could be that your communication isn't explicit enough about what you need, who needs to provide it, and when they need to provide it by.

 # TURNING IT AROUND

Right-size the communication to the audiences

For each of your audiences, make sure that your communication is very crisp, relevant, and timely to the audience. I don't expect a busy executive to read a detailed documentation on how a product function is to be designed, so I don't send it to him or her. For every communication that you send, make it worth their time to read it. If they don't need it, don't send it.

Take some time to redefine your audiences and how to communicate with them

You may need to redefine your communication plan because your audiences have been poorly defined or misaligned with the type of communication that they need. Do this as soon as you see some warning signs that your communication isn't reaching the right people to avoid confusion escalating to a fever pitch.

Follow the plan

You've done a plan, now follow it. If you need to make some tweaks because an audience is being over- or under-communicated to, don't be afraid to do so. I've seen too many communication plans fall by the wayside because more "important" things come up. Communication is important; keep up with the plan.

Make requests explicit and easy to see

If requests go unanswered, make sure that they are explicit, easy to find, and clear as to what needs to be done, who needs to do it, and when it needs to be done by. Doing timely follow-ups on requests are also very helpful as your project team and audiences will get the message that you don't let requests linger and die.

 **TAKE AWAYS**

- Have a clear communication plan which appropriately communicates to all of your defined audience groups
- Keep communications crisp, relevant, and regular; tune the communications to the audience
- Follow the plan, particularly when things aren't going well

We Didn't Pay Attention to Project Risks and Management Issues

So your project is humming along and stuff is getting done. Then, out of the blue, a key unanticipated product design issue comes up. As the project manager, you assess the design issue as not having a schedule impact and let the one of the project team members work it out. The design issue doesn't go away because the project team member thinks that the project manager is driving issue resolution. Before you know it, the project is late because the design issue wasn't addressed when it should have been.

Project risk and issue management is one of the most lethal but easily overlooked aspects of successful project management. Risks and issues derail your plan and cause you to divert focus away from project activities. But, there's simply no avoiding them. If you've got a project you're going to have risks and issues.

Now would be a good time to define risks and issues. First, let's talk about risks. Have you ever done a project plan and documented assumptions that needed to occur for the project to be successful? These are the conditions in which you are relying on a specific outcome otherwise your project will not succeed. Because you are relying on the assumption having a specific outcome, the assumption presents a risk to the project if the outcome is different. For example, let's say you make an assumption that customers are going to be available for a minimum of 20 hours per week throughout the project. Because you have made this assumption, you are relying on them to be available or there will be a negative impact to schedule. So, this assumption then becomes a project risk that needs to be managed.

Project risks have several attributes, as follows:

- They are generally known at the beginning of the project
- They can exist at a specific point in the project or can persist through the life of the project
- They can materially impact the outcome of the project if the risk comes true
- There is a reasonable likelihood that the risk could come true

- They are extraordinary to what would normally be managed on a project

Using your assumptions to identify the project risks is a very reasonable means of fleshing out the things on a project that are likely to hurt you. It is important, though, to focus on the important risks based on three factors: materiality, likelihood, and extraordinary-ness. When I define risks, I try to limit the risks to the top 6-8 things that have a likelihood of occurring, are extraordinary to normal project management, and could seriously hurt my project if they came true. As an example, if we were implementing a new technology I would absolutely have that as a project risk as there is a likelihood that the technology could fail and that it would seriously impact the project if it did indeed fail. I would not include risks like "activities must be completed on time" because, while it's material and likely, it's not extraordinary.

After you define your top project risks, your next step is to put mitigation strategies in place for each risk should the risk start coming true. So, if we take our example on implementing a new technology being a project risk, a mitigation strategy for the risk might include conducting stress and acceptance testing at the beginning of the project to ensure that the technology is able to perform under expected volumes. By defining mitigation strategies for each risk, you actively outline how you're going to head off the risk and manage away the potential problem. We'll discuss how risks are statused in the Screw-up #11—We didn't understand and report progress against the plan.

Precision in defining risks is very important. I once worked with a project manager who consistently said, "This project is risky." That statement, while it may be true, is completely unactionable in that I didn't know what to do to mitigate the risk. Your risks should be defined in terms of the action that needs to be taken to mitigate the risk. If you're unable to articulate the action, your risk is ill-defined or not a material risk.

Now, let's focus on management issues. Similar to project risks, issues are problems that occur on a project and need some management action for resolution. If an issue isn't addressed, it could materially impact successful completion of the project. Where issues differ from risks, however, is that they generally don't persist throughout the project and they may not be known at the onset of a project. Your issue list will not be persistent like your project risks; items will open and close as they are identified and resolved. What's important in managing issues is that the issue needs to be material to successful project completion to be a management issue. For example, a management issue exists if there is a policy decision that needs to be made as a precursor to a key design point being finalized and the decision needs to be made by the project sponsor. There's materiality because the policy change directly impacts the design and may have widespread impact on the organization. In addition, an item may be escalated to a management-level issue if the issue owner is unable or unwilling to drive resolution to the issue. In this situation, the project manager escalates the issue for the project sponsor or steering committee to help the issue owner resolve the issue.

When an issue makes it onto the management issue list, a desired result is documented along with an issue owner and a date in which the issue needs resolution. We'll discuss how issues are statused in Screw-up #11.

 **HOW IT HAPPENS**

Project risks or management issues don't get defined or don't focus on the important stuff

In defining project risks or management issues, it's important to ensure that the entire management team has input to and buys off on the lists. In defining risks, continue to ask yourself the following:

- Is it material if it happens?
- Is it likely to happen?
- Is it extraordinary versus just normal project management?

Similarly, when raising management issues, keep focus on materiality and project impact. It's also super-important to only raise issues to management after they exceed your span of control. If you chronically raise issues that the steering committee or project sponsor feels you should have been able to resolve on your own, your credibility as a project manager becomes suspect.

Project risks are defined but there is no mitigation strategy to manage through the risk

Defining and filtering your risk list is easy relative to defining mitigation strategies to navigate the risks. The mitigation strategies are going to be where your creativity and resourcefulness as a project manager come into play and, in my view, are one of the more fun parts of the job. I was running a project recently where we were deploying a new planning product and had an abnormally compressed timeframe to meet the needed completion date. We identified this as a key risk and employed as a mitigation weekly "show me's" where the product development team conducted weekly demonstrations of product functions completed that week. It worked great in that the product development team moved along quickly in order to meet their scheduled demonstrations, the project team got to see the weekly progress, and the team was able to react quickly if there was a problem with the product. Yes, this was an unconventional approach, but, given the identified risk, was a very appropriate and effective mitigation strategy.

Management issues are documented but there's no defined action to manage through the issues

Over the years, I've worked with a number of people who were great at saying, "I've got an issue" but did little beyond that to help resolve the issue. They are adept at backing up the issue dump truck into your project backyard, dumping the issues, and driving away leaving you to clean up the issue mess. As a project manager, I've learned to push back on issue dump truck drivers not only in clearly defining the issue, but also in being part of the resolution. Putting a thoughtful and concise action plan down with needed actions, dates, and owners is crucial to ensuring that management issues get closed before they fatally impact your project.

 **WARNING SIGNS**

You don't have a project risk or issue list

If you can't go to a place where risks and issues are readily handy and accessible by the project team, you're likely to get surprised by an issue or risk on the project.

You don't have a plan for how you would mitigate risks from coming true

If you've only documented risks and have no specific mitigation plan for each risk, you're just a sitting duck waiting for a risk to blow your project out of the water. Each material, likely, and extraordinary risk needs a clear mitigation to help ensure that the risk doesn't come true.

There's no clear owner or need date for resolving issues

An issue rears its head on the project, and because there isn't a clear date or singular owner for resolving it, a major budget or schedule impact is created on the project because the issue wasn't addressed on a timely basis. Each issue needs an owner and a date in which it needs to be resolved to keep things moving along.

The project sponsor or steering committee isn't utilized effectively for resolving issues

Either issues are escalated when they shouldn't be or issues aren't escalated when they should. You've likely got limited time with your sponsor or steering committee and you need to make sure that their time is spend on issues that you cannot control or require approval greater than you can provide.

TURNING IT AROUND

Get your risks defined and define clear mitigation strategies for each risk

It's never too late to take this step in your project. Take the time to think about the risks you face that are material, extraordinary, and likely. If you developed an assumptions list as part of your project plan, use that as a starting point. Review them with the project team to ensure that the list is right. Then put together very clear mitigation strategies for averting each risk. The best way to do this is to incorporate the mitigation activities in the project plan so they are a normal part of the project and not superfluous activities.

Right-size the issue list

Get clear about defining which issues the project team can resolve and which issues you need help from your sponsor, steering committee, or other stakeholder to resolve. Don't escalate issues that you can deal with amongst the project team

Know who's on the hook

For risks, make sure that there is an owner on the team for managing the mitigation. For issues, make sure that a team member owns teeing up the issue and proposed resolution with the project sponsor or steering committee. While the sponsor or steering committee is responsible for making the decision, the project team is responsible for analyzing alternatives and providing a recommendation.

 **TAKE AWAYS**

- Define your project risks from your assumptions list
- Focus on the important risks and issues
- Don't just say "The project is risky;" explain what the risks are and then develop a mitigation strategy to address each risk
- Be diligent about identifying action plans for issues including actions, dates and owners

Screw-up
#10

**The Project
Cost Much
More Than
Expected**

In writing this chapter, I struggled quite a bit with whether or not this was a screw-up. I have done a number of projects where the end result was successful but the money spent on the project was more than originally anticipated. So, is that screw-up? From a project delivery perspective, it may or may not be a screw-up considering your particular culture. However, from the perspective of establishing your credibility as a project manager who is able to estimate and deliver a project within agreed-upon funding, it most certainly is a screw-up. Your ability to complete a project on time and on budget is a critical gauge to your continued success as a project manager.

As with other topics in this book, there are a number of very good books written on managing project costs so I'm not going to go in-depth on cost management techniques here. What I will do, though, is touch upon some of the problems that I've encountered in managing a project budget and some techniques that may be helpful in managing the problems.

First, let's lock on some project-costing terminology to ensure that we're on the same page:

- **Total budget**—the budgeted amount that has been authorized for the project

- **Current budget**—the amount that has been budgeted to date on the project

- **Actual spent**—the amount that has been spent to date on the project

- **Remaining budget**—total budget minus current budget

- **Current variance**—the variance between current budget and actual spent

- **Estimate to complete forecast**—the amount you plan on spending from the actual spend point to the end of the project

- **Estimate to complete variance**—the variance between the remaining budget and the estimate to complete forecast

- **Estimate at completion**—actual amount spent plus estimate to complete forecast
- **Estimate at completion variance**—the variance between the total budget for the project and the estimate at completion
- **Budgeted contingency**—a fund added to the project to accommodate unplanned activities.
- **Remaining contingency**—the amount of contingency funds left after unplanned activity withdrawals.

At any point in time on a project, you as the project manager should know each of these numbers to effectively know if your project costs are being managed effectively. Now, some of you may be a bit skeptical at this point and may be thinking that this is just project over-administration. Let's look briefly at how these cost indicators interact to give you a complete cost picture on your project.

Let's take an example of a three-month project that has a total budget of $100,000 with $10,000 of budgeted contingency built into the project. You are currently three weeks into the project and at this point have actually spent $30,000 in total against a current budget of $30,000. The project now has a current variance of $0. Things look OK, right? Let me give you a bit more information. Of the $10,000 in budgeted contingency, $5,000 was spent on unplanned activities, which leaves $5,000 in remaining contingency. The estimate to complete forecast is $80,000 because the unplanned activities are going to add work to the rest of the project. So, the estimate at completion is the actual spend of $30,000 plus the estimate to complete forecast of $80,000, which equals an estimate at completion of $110,000 versus a total budget of $100,000. So, if I am just looking at current variance during week three the project looks great, but if I look at where the project will end I've got at least a $10,000 estimate at completion variance that I'm definitely going to incur. Depending on your environment, $10,000 may or may not be a big issue, but hopefully you see the problem.

HOW IT HAPPENS

The project estimate at completion variance isn't managed

When managing project costs, it's not only important to know where you stand right now, but it's also important to know where you're going to end up. When you look at estimate at completion, it forces you to look holistically at your project to include all your incurred and anticipated project costs to come up with an accurate estimate at completion. In my early years, I did projects where my estimate at complete variance continued to grow week by week because I didn't have an accurate estimate to complete forecast. I then had a big surprise on my hands when my project came in much more over budget than I anticipated.

The project actual resource mix is different from the budgeted resource mix

In building up your cost estimate, you likely made assumptions about the types of resources that you would need and the relative cost of each resource. Too many times, though, I've gotten caught up in having a different resource mix than I planned. More often than not, the actual resource mix was more expensive than the budgeted resource mix. Thus, I had a budget problem that got worse as the project continued so long as I continued the project with the more expensive resource mix. It's kind of like watching a tidal wave coming at you and getting bigger and bigger as it is about to engulf you.

The project didn't plan for or manage a contingency fund

When estimating project costs, I will typically include a contingency fund that adds between 10-20% to the total project cost.

This number can vary based on the following factors:

- The number, magnitude, and nature of identified project risks
- The degree of learning curve that the project team will incur
- The open issues that are known at project inception

Many project managers I have seen in the past were good at establishing a contingency fund and taking into account the factors I have outlined above. When things fell apart, though, the project manager lost focus on managing the contingency fund and knowing the remaining contingency. As a project manager, it's important to know how the contingency fund is being spent; for example, are activity withdrawals happening due to unplanned work or inefficiencies in completing planned work? If you're consuming contingency on activities that you didn't expect would consume contingency, then you are likely to have a cost surprise when an unplanned activity does hit your project.

The project manager's request for additional funding isn't credible

When you do have the unfortunate situation where you have to go back for additional funding, several things are critical in developing a credible additional funding request:

- Have a very clear story on why the overrun has occurred.
- Look at your remaining activities to see if something can be cut as a trade-off to spending additional dollars, which gives the project sponsor choices in either reducing the scope of the product or spending additional money.
- Have a very clear, credible and realistic estimate at completion for each trade-off.
- Make the request as inclusive as possible to avoid subsequent unplanned requests.

- Don't plan on silver bullets to save your budget; make sure you truly believe in the numbers and you're not kidding yourself.

- Be honest about what assumptions did not "pan out." You will look more credible.

Simply put, going back to ask for more money isn't fun. In fact, I've found it to be one of the more humbling aspects of my job, particularly if I could have done some things to better avert the overrun.

 **WARNING SIGNS**

Your current variance keeps growing as the project goes on

If your current variance grows legs and continues to get larger week after week, you've most likely got a budget problem on your hands. Variances that trend in the wrong direction most likely continue to trend in that direction if left unchecked.

You have to do more unplanned work than you originally anticipated

Unplanned work will mean unplanned costs. You may have enough to cover for this in your contingency fund, but unless you're actively managing your contingency fund you could end up with a cost overrun.

You don't know how much contingency you've consumed and what it was consumed on

Being on budget without knowing the status of your contingency fund is, in my view, no better than a cost overrun. You may get lucky and not need any more of your contingency, but better that you know for sure what your contingency fund was used for and know if there are likely to be further withdrawals.

Your current variance fluctuates but your estimate to complete variance stays at zero

Instability in your historical variance is likely to mean that variance fluctuation will continue with future tasks. If you're running an unfavorable current variance yet your estimate to complete variance shows you being on budget, you're probably kidding yourself. Understanding history on your project is a great way to forecast the future of the project.

 # TURNING IT AROUND

Get a grip on your cost situation

Start by getting a really good understanding of current variance and your contingency fund. After you understand history, get a good view of your forecast. Being realistic and inclusive is super-critical here, but don't go overboard with padding the forecast. Excessive padding can lead to your estimate not being credible in the eyes of your sponsor or steering committee.

Understand what tradeoffs you can make on remaining work

As a business owner, I appreciated it when a project manager gave me choices and clearly outlined the consequences for each choice. My decision between choosing between dropping product features to stay within budget versus incurring a cost overrun could be different depending on factors either inside or outside the project. As an example, I may or may not have contingency funds that I can use to cover the cost overrun or I may decide to bite the bullet and spend the extra money because the product features are important enough for me to pay extra for them.

Minimize the number of times you ask for more money

I've found that each time I go back to the well with a new request, my credibility as a project manager erodes exponentially. When asking for additional money I strive to do a single request and make my request as inclusive as possible. If there are some unknown factors on the project that could cause the project to include additional requests, I like to include those factors in my contingency and then provide a contingency status depending on the outcome of the unknown factors. As I said earlier, make sure that your request is explicit and credible. Don't go crazy with padding the numbers.

 **TAKE AWAYS**

- Manage to estimate at completion variance, not just current variance

- Plan for a contingency fund for unanticipated activities and manage withdrawals from the contingency fund

- Minimize the number of times that you go back to the well for more money

We Didn't
Understand and
Report Progress
Against the Plan

Pilots have always amazed me. There's the sheer knowledge that a pilot needs to have just to know what all those little buttons, lights, and toggle switches do. There are the pre-flight planning and checklists they go through to make sure they travel safely. There's the tight communication they need to have with air and ground traffic control to make sure they don't crash into another plane. The thing that amazes me most, though, is their ability to keep things under control when unexpected things happen such as turbulence or a mechanical failure. One flight I was on a number of years ago hit some terrible wind shear. I was sitting in the last row and had just been served a cup of coffee. When the wind shear hit, the iron bird felt more like a roller coaster than a plane. By the time we got through the wind shear, my coffee cup was empty, there were coffee drops on the ceiling, and the passenger in front of me was now wearing a multi-colored shirt. Just as we were about to hit the wind shear, the pilot came on the PA system with this calm, re-assuring Robert Young-like voice (again, I'm dating myself) telling us that we were going to have "a bit" of turbulence ahead. Immediately after we got through the turbulence, that same calm voice came on letting us know that we were through it and that it looked to be smooth skies ahead. I was so glad to know there was someone at the helm who was focused and determined to get us through the turbulence and to our destination.

Managing a project plan is similar to a pilot flying a plane from origin to destination. The project manager needs to know the project's status at all times, know what things are happening around the project that can affect its outcome, and must be calm and prescriptive when project wind shear hits.

A major consideration in managing to the plan is the ability to understand and communicate the project's status throughout the life of the project. But why bother with status reporting? After all, time spent doing project administration is better spent working on "real" tasks, right? *Bzzzzzzzzzzzzzzt*, take a seat, you don't win the Tappan microwave. Doing an effective status report doesn't have to be a mundane, laborious, non-value-added project activity. In fact, I've found that the more concise your status report, the more effective it is at communicating where you are to your stakeholders. Over the years, I have zeroed in on my status report by focusing on four key management areas:

- Schedule Management
- Risk Management
- Issue Management
- Cost Management

First, let's define what project utopia means. To me, it means that we are on schedule on all our critical and non-critical path activities, we are under on costs, there are no management-level issues needing resolution, and all risks we have identified have not come true. I'd love to meet the project manager that got to live in utopia-land from a project start-to-finish. I've certainly never been that fortunate. So anything that causes you to slip from utopia now becomes turbulence that you have to fly through.

From a schedule perspective, I place very strong focus on what the critical path is through the project. It's this critical path that I watch like a hawk and manage tightly to ensure that the project stays on schedule. This doesn't mean, though, that you can relax on non-critical path activities. On complex projects with highly interdependent activities, it is common for the critical path chain to change as activities get completed. As the project manager, you need to understand the activity interdependencies, know when the critical path through the project is about to change, and ensure that the project team understands the critical path chain. I've heard some project managers say things like, "Yeah, the critical path through my project is design, development, testing, and implementation." And just to think that someone went to college to learn that. Understanding the detail is knowing the lowest level of activities in your activity breakdown that have less than a 40-hour duration and have a single name assigned to them. You absolutely need to understand things at that level if you're going to deftly navigate through turbulence.

In understanding project schedule progress, I've found it very important to keep the project schedule very current and relevant but at the same time avoid nagging the project team for status on activities. I've found that doing a general status on work activities at least weekly is a good rule of thumb. By status, you're primarily focused on how much more work needs to be done on an activity before the activity can be called complete (commonly referred to as *estimate to complete* or ETC). It's critical to stress with your team members that reality is paramount when assessing ETC. As I've worked with different teams over the years, I've been able to classify team members into three categories when getting ETCs; the realists, the dreamers, and the sandbaggers. The realists are those that are able to give a very accurate estimate to complete and carry a high degree of credibility. The dreamers will generally err on the side of being too aggressive with their ETCs and will chronically miss their dates even if they just one day prior insisted that they were going to hit their date. The sandbaggers will generally err on the side of being too pessimistic and give you a padded date to help "manage your expectations." I love working with realists and am equally frustrated with dreamers and sandbaggers. When I know that someone is a dreamer or sandbagger my tendency is to drill down more on their estimates because they don't have the degree of credibility that the realist has.

When ETCs are plugged into the schedule and you've assessed whether you're ahead, behind, or on schedule, it's important to discuss progress in a status meeting and produce a status report. I'm very focused on doing status meetings at least bi-weekly and strongly feel that a representative from each of the project roles should be at the status meetings. I like to run very structured one-hour status meetings with a standing agenda, as follows:

1. A brief review of any product features that were developed in the prior week

2. A review and status of the schedule and assessment of the critical path chain

3. A review and status of each material project risk

4. A review and status of material project issues that require management focus

5. A review and status of project costs and adherence to budget

In reviewing developed product features, I believe it's crucial that the team sees the progress that is being made on a project to build and maintain momentum. On one recent project, we had one of the developers demonstrate some feature that was developed in the last week. Everyone knew that the feature was a work-in-process and didn't get too upset if an occasional problem occurred (except if it was supposed to be "complete"—see previous for "dreamers"). Showing regular progress is a huge psychological boost for the team.

In reviewing schedule, the project manager provides his/her assessment of critical path activities. I've found that physically walking the team through the critical path chain is very helpful in ensuring that everyone understands the schedule status of the project and the points where there is likely to be project turbulence. The status gets summarized into a "Key Milestones Status," which looks like the following:

Key Milestones Status					
Status	**Milestone**	**Owner**	**Key Dates**		
			Plan	**Revised**	**Actual**
↑	Assemble project team	Dawn Jones	11/27		11/27
	Complete design specifications	Kent O'Brien	12/15	12/17	12/17
↓	Complete order management development	Michelle Stephens	2/18	2/28	
→	Complete shipping management development	Peg McNichol	2/28	3/5	
→	Complete technical testing	Dale Fleming	4/1	4/11	
↑	Complete user acceptance testing	Bonnie Dentz	5/1		
→	Complete training	Bonnie Dentz	5/15	5/25	
→	Implement system	Paul Brennan	5/22	6/1	

In characterizing status, I like to use a red/yellow/green type of coding scheme, as follows:

- **Green**—The milestone will be completed on schedule.
- **Yellow**—There is a potential slip in the milestone. The project team is taking steps to mitigate the potential milestone slip.
- **Red**—The potential for a slip is realized and unless immediate action is taken the milestone will slip its scheduled completion.

In this example, the first two tasks have been completed on 11/27 and 12/17, respectively. The complete order shipping management development task is at risk of slipping from 2/28 to 3/5, but the team is working to pull the date back to its planned completion date. The order management development task is at significant risk to meet its 2/18 planned completion, and unless the team is able to re-arrange work, the milestone will slip. The slips in the development tasks then put subsequent milestones at risk and require the project team to see where work can be re-arranged to keep things on schedule.

Recall from Screw-up #9 our discussion on material risks. I like to summarize and track risks using the following grid:

Project Risks			
Indicator	Risk	Mitigation	Owner
↑	1. Developers are unfamiliar with new technology	Employ consultants through development phase to supplement team expertise	Dawn Jones
↑	2. Customers are not available for the project team per the project schedule	Provide two-week look-aheads on meeting schedules and confirm customer attendance for each meeting	Bonnie Dentz
→	3. New technology cannot handle expected volumes	Conduct stress testing on new technology with anticipated volumes to ensure acceptable performance	Kent O'Brien

In characterizing risk status, I use a red/yellow/green coding scheme similar to schedule status, as follows:

- **Green**—everything is OK with the risk.
- **Yellow**—there are signs that the risk is about to come true and increased emphasis needs to be placed on the mitigation.
- **Red**—the risk is happening and the risk will cause a project impact unless immediate action is taken.

In the previous example, risk #3 is showing signs that the risk is about to come true. Initial stress testing on the product is yielding unfavorable results. Additional focus is being placed on the risk to see if it can be pulled back to a green status.

Similarly, I summarize issues in the same manner, shown as follows:

Management Issues Requiring Attention					
Indicator	Key Issue	Desired Resolution	Owner	Need by	Status
→	1. Decision required on whether orders can be accepted without an accompanying purchase order	Permit placement of orders without customer entering a purchase order number	Bonnie Dentz	2/1	In Process
↓	2. Customer manager is being refocused on other activities from her home organization	Re-obtain commitment from home organization on assignment; utilize exec sponsor if necessary	Dawn Jones	1/10	In Process
↑	3. Project is unable to get dedicated training environment for system	Obtain commitment from IT management that separate environment can be secured	Kent O'Brien	1/15	Closed

In characterizing issue status, I use the same red/yellow/green coding scheme:

- **Green**—The issue has been closed without impacting the project.
- **Yellow**—The issue has been identified, and unless the owner resolves by the needed date, the project will be impacted.
- **Red**—The issue hasn't been resolved and there will be an impact to the project until it is resolved.

In this example, issue number 1 is in the process of being resolved with Bonnie Dentz needing to resolve it by 2/1. Issue number 2 has not been resolved by 1/10 and the project will have an adverse impact until it is resolved. Issue number 3 has just been closed satisfactorily and will roll off the management issue list on the next status report.

On costs, I like to base my overall assessment on my estimate at completion variance, as shown here:

Project Costs			
Indicator	Total Budget	Estimate at Completion	Variance
↑	$500,000	$485,000	$15,000(f)

For my cost indicator I use the following scheme:

- **Green**—The estimate at completion variance is favorable.
- **Yellow**—The estimate at completion variance is unfavorable and we're assessing whether an additional funding decision will be needed.
- **Red**—The estimate at completion variance is unfavorable and the project will not be completed successfully without additional funding or reduction in scope.

When you have all of the detail in the status report completed, it is helpful to write a brief executive summary (no more than a half-page). In writing the summary, I try to focus on describing the rationale for each indicator and also use it as means to give particular acknowledgement for any over-and-above efforts that the team or business partner groups are giving towards the project. I've found that, particularly when the project is going through rough times, it is important to acknowledge those who are making significant contribution to the project. The executive summary looks as follows:

Overall Status	Schedule	Risks	Issues	Cost
	↓	→	↓	↑

Key components of order management and shipping modules were reviewed with minor revisions requested by the customer. At this point, schedule is in a red status due to a 10-day slippage in work on the order management development completion. The project team is assessing alternatives to bringing in schedule via supplementing with additional resources and working overtime. If we are unable to recover, schedule downstream activities will be assessed to mitigate overall project slippage. Risks are at yellow status due to initial unfavorable stress testing results; subsequent test is being conducted to validate initial results. Issues are at red status due to customer manager being pulled from project to work on other activities. Request has been placed with home organization and the project sponsor for help. Project costs are green with estimate at completion being in line with total budget for project.The project team is doing an outstanding job of working through some difficult issues and working to keepproject tasks on schedule to the best of their ability. Particular thanks to the technical groups supporting the project for working overtime to help keep things on schedule.

So, if we put the entire status report together, it looks like this:

Order Management & Shipping System Status Report
As Of: 1/12/20xx

Overall Status	Schedule	Risks	Issues	Cost
	↓	→	↓	↑

Key components of order management and shipping modules were reviewed with minor revisions requested by customers. At this point, schedule is in a red status due to a 10-day slippage in work on the order management development completion. The project team is assessing alternatives to bringing in schedule via supplementing with additional resources and working overtime. If we are unable to recover, schedule downstream activities will be assessed to mitigate overall project slippage. Risks are at yellow status due to initial unfavorable stress testing results; subsequent test is being conducted to validate initial results. Issues are at red status due to customer manager being pulled from project to work on other activities. Request has been placed with home organization and the project sponsor for help. Project costs are green with estimate at completion being in line with total budget for project.The project team is doing an outstanding job of working through some difficult issues and working to keep project tasks on schedule to the best of their ability. Particular thanks to the technical groups supporting the project for working overtime to help keep things on schedule.

Key Milestones Status					
				Key Dates	
Status	Milestone	Owner	Plan	Revised	Actual
⊘	Assemble project team	Dawn Jones	11/27		11/27
⊘	Complete design specifications	Kent O Brien	12/15	12/17	12/17
Œ	Complete order management development	Michelle Stephens	2/18	2/28	
Ŀ	Complete shipping management development	Peg McNichol	2/28	3/5	
Ŀ	Complete technical testing	Dale Fleming	4/1	4/11	
⊘	Complete user acceptance testing	Bonnie Dentz	5/1		
Ŀ	Complete training	Bonnie Dentz	5/15	5/25	
Ŀ	Implement system	Paul Brennan	5/22	6/1	

Project Risks			
Indicator	Risk	Mitigation	Owner
⊘	1. Developers are unfamiliar with new technology	Employ consultants through development phase to supplement team expertise	Dawn Jones
⊘	2. Customers are not available for the project team per the project schedule	Provide two-week look-aheads on meeting schedules and confirm customer attendance for each meeting	Bonnie Dentz
Ŀ	3. New technology cannot handle expected volumes	Conduct stress testing on new technology with anticipated volumes to ensure acceptable performance	Kent O Brien

Management Issues Requiring Attention					
Indicator	Key Issue	Desired Resolution	Owner	Need by	Status
Ŀ	1. Decision required on whether orders can be accepted without an accompanying purchase order	Permit placement of orders without customer entering a purchase order number	Bonnie Dentz	2/1	In Process
Œ	2. Customer project manager is being refocused on other activities from her home organization	Re-obtain commitment from home organization on assignment; utilize exec sponsor if necessary	Dawn Jones	1/10	In Process
⊘	3. Project is unable to get dedicated training environment for system	Obtain commitment from IT management that separate environment can be secured	Kent O Brien	1/15	Closed

Project Costs			
Indicator	Total Budget	Estimate at Completion	Variance
⊘	$500,000	$485,000	$15,000(f)

OK, now that you've seen the entire status report, here are some additional thoughts:

- This looks like a lot of information and your initial view might be that it would be a pain to complete every week. I've been very successful on multiple projects with completing the status report during the status meeting by starting with the prior week's status and modifying as necessary. I literally would send out the status report to stakeholders at the end of the team status meeting.

- The red/yellow/green statuses may need to be customized for your environment and culture. Just try to stick to the following general theme:
  - Green = Good
  - Yellow = Potential problems
  - Red = Big problems
- You may need to adapt some sections to better align with your environment; feel free to do so, just be cautious of making the status report too difficult, voluminous, or cumbersome to follow.

HOW IT HAPPENS

Progress against the schedule isn't tracked or is not kept up to date

Putting a great schedule together is great, but poor tracking against the schedule renders the plan as ineffective in helping you get the project done. I've seen quite a few projects go sideways because the project manager either wasn't enforcing adherence to the schedule or didn't keep schedule activities current.

Weekly team meetings aren't held

Having very structured project management team meetings which review product features, schedule, risks, issues and costs are paramount to making sure that your project team is in the know and that everyone is focused on the right priorities. Getting together for one hour a week to do this is time very well spent to ensure that your project management team understands where the project is and knows what things are happening that might affect them.

Status reports aren't prepared or aren't timely

Equally important to conducting status meetings is preparing formal, timely, accurate, and concise status reports. It doesn't have to take a tremendous amount of time to do — as I mentioned earlier, I usually completed the status report in our status meetings projected on a screen for everyone to see what I was writing. You also want to avoid having your status reports contain stale information. I worked on one project where status reports would go out every Wednesday but they would have an "as of" date of the previous Friday. Thus, any activity that happened on Monday and Tuesday would not be reflected in the status report. This can be very frustrating, particularly if you're dealing with hot issues where the issue has either escalated or been resolved in between the time of the status report as of date and the date it was sent out.

Action isn't taken quickly when problems crop up

When a status indicator changes to yellow it is your cue as a project manager to take action. Your job here is to make sure that

- There is someone on point to address the problem
- There is some expectation of what needs to be done to address the problem
- There is a date that the problem needs to be resolved
- There is regular follow-up on the status of the problem
- The problem only goes away when it is resolved

In your role as project manager, your follow-up ability will be key in holding people accountable for getting problems resolved. If your team knows that you are going to publicly follow up with assigned members on the status of problems, they are much more likely to focus on diligently resolving the problems.

WARNING SIGNS

You're getting questions about the progress of the project from stakeholders or team members

Frequent questions like "Where are we?" from project team members or stakeholders is a pretty good indicator that you're not communicating the project status as frequently as necessary or in a concise manner. This is not only frustrating for the stakeholder or team member, but also randomizes the project manager by having to field one-off requests for information.

The project team isn't clear on the problems that the project is currently facing

Project team members being surprised or confused by problems likely means that timely communication isn't happening or that the warning signals aren't in place for early problem identification. It could also mean that the team isn't meeting frequently enough to corporately understand the problem and the alternatives to resolving it.

Problems don't have a clear owner or "resolution needed-by" date

Problems assigned to "the team" or to some other group of people might just as well not be assigned at all, because it is unlikely that someone will take ownership for resolving the problem. Each problem, whether it is a schedule, issue, risk, or cost issue needs to be assigned to a singular owner with a needed-by date.

You don't know when something is about to be a problem

If you're frequently surprised by problems hitting you without any advanced warning, you might not have the right early warning system in place to identify potential problems so that you can take timely action. Surprises are fun for birthday parties, not so fun for projects.

TURNING IT AROUND

Get real with the schedule

Make sure that your project schedule tasks accurately reflect the work that is being done, the team member assigned to the work, and the scheduled start and complete dates for the task. If the schedule contains stale data, you're very likely to make stakeholders and team members nervous that no one is at the controls and to erode your credibility in reporting accurate status of the project.

Listen for trains

Make use of a yellow status to understand where something might be going sideways so that you can take deliberate action. If you see that key project indicators frequently go from green to red, you're waiting for the train to be right on top of you before you decide to move off the tracks.

Keep it simple

Don't require that someone spend a lot of time trying to understand the status report. Use symbols, colors, and concise verbiage to communicate where things are. On projects where I have been the project sponsor, I would first look at the top of the status report to see what the key indicators were for schedule, risks, issues, and cost. If I saw all green arrows, I skimmed the rest of the status. If I saw any yellow or red, I would drill down deeper on the affected area.

Get trackin'

Be very diligent about tracking progress against your plan and getting very accurate ETCs for each of your in-process activities on a weekly basis. Make sure that you have a strong understanding of your critical path chain and that you know when the critical path has changed. Also, resist the temptation to abandon the project plan when things start going sideways on a project. You need to be firmly at the controls making sure that the plan represents reality and not some pipe dream.

 **TAKE AWAYS**

- Do weekly team status meetings to review product feature progress, progress against milestones, risk, issues, and costs.
- Always know the critical path through the project.
- Don't let the project schedule get out of date; always know who is supposed to be doing what task and where they are with completing the task.
- Send out a status report immediately after the status meeting.
- Ensure that content is credible; if things are going badly, own up to it; don't cover things up.
- Know who can help you with mitigating risks and addressing issues; get them involved early.
- Be diligent about addressing problems early; don't assume they'll go away or fix themselves.

We Tried To Do Too Much

As a consultant, I was trained very early on to focus on delighting my client. As one partner told me, "It's not the partners who promote you to partner, it's your clients who promote you to partner." As a very young and eager project manager, I took the "delight the client" mantra very seriously and would do just about anything for my client. All they had to do was ask me, and as long as I could do the work and not have a budget overrun, I would do it. This all worked out great until it caught up with me at one particular client.

I had a project team of six people working on a major enhancement to a computer system. The team was working long hours to get the work done and was already on edge. The client then asked me if I could take on another project to set up a separate training environment for the computer system. In my "delight the client" mentality, I worked up an estimate of the work and drew up an arrangement letter to set up the environment for $15,000. The client accepted and I reveled in the fact that I had, indeed, gone one more step to delighting the client. Then I turned to the team and asked them to get this work done in addition to the other project. It's a miracle that I'm here to write about this today as I thought they were going to burn me at the stake. I shrugged off their concerns and told them that setting up the environment would be no big deal and that they could get it done in a couple of days. They gave me a "clueless manager" glance and said that they would do the best they could. This story ended with both projects slipping their schedules, two people quitting, one very ticked off client, one very very ticked off client partner (my boss), and one very humbled project manager. What started off as "delighting the client" ended up as a disaster because I over-committed the team by trying to do too much.

What causes a project team to take on too much work? I've seen several factors:

- A desire to delight the client, management or the customer by giving them everything they want and then some
- An overzealous project manager who sees personal gain in taking on more work
- An unrealistic customer or project sponsor who trivializes additions in scope with phrases like "This is so easy, I could do it"
- A legitimate change request that is taken on as additional scope without understanding tradeoffs of other in-scope items

As I discussed in Screw-up #2, it's crucial for a project manager to ensure that the scope of the project is very clear, concise, and doable from the onset and that changes and tradeoffs in scope are managed thoughtfully. So, how do you know if you're doing too much? Here are some questions to help you make that determination:

- Does the scope of the work span more than one project sponsor?
- Can you clearly articulate the business problem you're trying to solve and have a concise project mission statement?
- Is it difficult to develop a one-page scope slide that articulates what you're trying to do?
- Are you trying to fix some things that aren't broken with the things that are broken?
- Are you having difficulty drawing and enforcing scope boundaries?

In looking at your project, you need to be very cognizant about keeping the team from doing too much. The team is relying on you as the project manager to protect them from failure by knowing when to say no.

HOW IT HAPPENS

Project scope isn't set or controlled appropriately

Scope creep can very quickly turn a well-structured project into a failed project. The really difficult thing about scope creep is, just as the name implies, it "creeps" up on you. Sure, it may only take a day or so of development time to complete an additional product enhancement, but when you add up ten or twenty product enhancements plus the overhead of testing and training, you've now added significant pieces of work to the project.

At the same time, you need to take caution in setting your scope so narrowly and putting on blinders that you don't meet the original mission statement. You may find that when you first define a mission statement you think that you are addressing the business problem but later discover that you've underscoped the project.

The project team doesn't know when to say 'good enough'

It's great to have a motivated and exuberant project team. I've continually been amazed at how much work a well-oiled project team can churn out in a limited timeframe. As the project manager, you need to keep check on the exuberance factor to make sure that the team doesn't materially increase the project scope. I've seen this happen particularly as the project team sees the end product taking shape and is able to envision how the product could meet the customer need. A key tip-off for me is when someone starts off with something like "Wouldn't it be cool if the product did <put product enhancement here>." I'm not advocating that an automatic "no" comes from your mouth because it very well could be a great idea. It just needs to follow the change review board process and needs to be controlled work that is managed just like any other project activity.

The team attempts to fill available hours of capacity with additional work

The primary objective of your project is to meet the customer need within the agreed-upon schedule and budget constraints. The objective of the project is not to keep each project team member fully utilized through the end of the project. I've seen many project teams break product functionality just prior to release because they have tried to squeeze in additional product enhancements at the last minute because someone had a few hours of capacity to do the work. Releasing a stable product that is reliable and predictable with a few less bells and whistles is far more important than an unstable, unreliable product that has bells and whistles and may or may not work.

 **WARNING SIGNS**

You hear too many "it would be great if the product did..." after product design is frozen

You could have a customer or an exuberant project team member wanting to add additional product features after you have already frozen your design. Some of the feature requests could be critical to support product function but could also be "nice to haves" which will not materially affect your product.

The project team is working too many hours

Sometimes working overtime is just a fact of life, but if you're seeing the project team working sustained periods of excessive overtime it could be a sign that there is simply too much work to do within the time you're trying to do it.

There's confusion about the scope of the project after product design is frozen

Getting a lot of scope questions after product design is frozen can lead to doing too much because the scope lines haven't been drawn clearly. When your scope lines aren't drawn clearly, you're more likely to include additional items in scope because you either missed something or because you don't have a strong basis to exclude something from scope.

 **TURNING IT AROUND**

Lock down the scope

If you see the scope as being poorly defined, re-calibrate the scope and assess the impact of what you're doing on cost and schedule. When a scope re-calibration is necessary, be very deliberate about the assessment and try to provide options to your project sponsor on what you could do within given cost and schedule constraints and what the additional cost and schedule impact would be if scope were to be increased.

Know when to say no

Sometimes you've just got to say no to additional work if it means the overall quality of the product is likely to be jeopardized. When determining your answer, consider the following:

- Is the additional feature absolutely essential to product functionality?
- What is the impact to the customer if the feature isn't included?
- Is the feature crucial enough to extend schedule and/or budget to get it done?

As I said earlier, I like to delight my customer, but at the same time I don't want to give them a sub-standard product because there was too much work to do.

Revise the project schedule and budget to accommodate change in scope

If the additional work is absolutely essential to the product, be deliberate about revising the schedule and budget to accommodate the increase in scope. Word of caution: If you're going to do a scope change, make sure that you are including all the areas of scope that are essential to develop an acceptable product. You don't want to have a repeat performance of revising your schedule and budget later in the project because of another scope issue. Get the lines drawn once, get them agreed upon with the project sponsor and the customer, and revise the schedule and budget accordingly.

 **TAKE AWAYS**

- Work diligently to control scope, but don't become myopic and draw scope lines too narrow
- Know when to say something is good enough; meet the objective but don't over-extend
- Resist filling every available hour of capacity with additional work

We Didn't Do
Enough Testing

As much as I enjoyed my elementary school years, there were few greater joys than the fire drill. The alarm invariably went off right in the middle of a very boring subject, and all the kids first let out a gleeful "oooooohhhhhh," walked (remember, never run) to the coat racks to get our coats, then headed outside in single file out to the playground. The teachers then took roll call to make sure everyone was accounted for. Then, after all was clear, we all walked back into the classroom, hung up our coats, and took our seats only to find out that we now had to complete the boring topic for homework....

This is one example of testing a process to ensure that everything that is supposed to happen does so as expected. Regardless of the product you are developing on your project, there will likely be some testing you will do to ensure that your product meets customer expectations.

I don't think any rational project manager would disagree that some testing is an important component in ensuring the final product functions as expected. What I have seen on many projects, though, is the testing process being condensed and truncated because other tasks prior to testing over-ran their scheduled time to complete. Rather than changing the completion date to reflect the overrun, many project managers will shorten the amount of testing that needs to be done to try to stay on schedule. Sometimes this is accomplished by adding additional resources to the testing process to gain back schedule. Other times, though, the product simply won't be tested adequately and the end customer will bear the brunt of discovering product defects.

Depending upon your product, the types and intensity of testing can vary dramatically. For critical parts that are purchased from a third party which will go into an aircraft, you may undergo destructive testing to ensure that the part can withstand acceptable levels of stress before breaking. For a change to an employee benefit package, you may undergo focus group testing to test the appeal and impact of the package. For a new system, you may undergo volume testing to ensure that the system meets technical performance requirements when processing real-life data volumes. There are as many ways to test as there are types of projects, but in this chapter I will lay out some fundamentals of testing that you can use which can apply to a wide range of projects.

HOW IT HAPPENS

There is no test plan

The best test plans that I have seen in my experience have the following components:

- A definition of the types of testing that need to occur on the product, such as unit testing, destructive testing, and customer acceptance testing
- A logical breakdown of your testing process into phases or cycles
- Desired outcomes that clearly demonstrate successful completion of each test
- Required people, time, and other resources needed to complete the testing

I am a co-owner in a prepared food service business. In determining menu items, we developed a test plan for how each entrée would be tested to determine if it should be on the final menu. During our first level of testing, which we called "alpha" testing, a small group of us prepared test entrees using different methods, such as boiling, microwaving, or baking, and evaluate the food for taste, consistency, uniqueness, profitability and ease of preparation on a scale of 1-10 with "10" being outstanding. If the entrée passed our alpha testing with a score of 9 or 10, we released the entrée to a small group of customer testers we called "beta" testers. They then prepared the entrées according to our specification and evaluated the food on three criteria: quality, convenience, and timesavings using a 1-10 rating scale for each. If the entrée scored a 9 or 10 in each of the categories and the customer was willing to pay a price close to our suggested retail price, the entrée passed beta testing and was put on the menu. Our testing of the entrées followed the above plan characteristics:

- We had a definition of the types of testing that needed to occur (boiling, microwaving, baking)
- We had a logical breakdown of the testing process into phases (alpha and beta testing)
- We had desired outcomes for each phase of testing (a score of 9-10 for taste, consistency, uniqueness, profitability and ease of preparation for alpha testing and quality, convenience, and time savings for beta testing)
- We had required resources for testing (cooking utensils, internal alpha testers, customer beta testers, and test entrées)

All these components helped us to ensure that we were look-ing at the right things in our entrées and also protected us from releasing entrées to our beta customer testers that were sub-standard. And it also gave us one tasty menu!

There is a plan but it isn't being followed

So there's a beautiful plan that is put together and has all the required testing types, a schedule which is clearly divided into cycles, expected results are clearly defined, and all the resource needs are outlined. The only problem is that the plan isn't fol-lowed because either there's not enough time to complete the required tests or the required resources aren't available at the beginning of testing. So, a nice piece of work goes largely unused and a haphazard job of testing is done in its place.

There isn't a clear definition of what success means

So how do you know that a test passed or failed and what do you do if it failed? In the preceding food service example, if the entrée failed alpha testing we rejected it from the menu completely. If it failed beta testing, we made an assessment of whether we could make any adjustments that might improve quality, convenience, or timesavings. If it made sense to make adjustments, we implemented the needed changes and re-submitted the entrée to the beta testers. If not, we rejected it from the menu completely. We knew what success meant and knew what to do on failure.

The customer isn't included in the testing

Regardless of the type of project I manage, I have a strong bias of somehow including the customer in the testing process. I am cautious to put a few things in place so that the customer testing experience is fruitful and relevant, as follows:

- Make sure that the internal team tests the product first to flesh out any obvious defects.
- Define a small, controlled, "friendly" customer group to do initial customer testing prior to releasing to a larger group of customers.
- Do controlled debriefs with your customer testers to give them an opportunity to give you very timely, relevant, and frank feedback on the product.
- Don't over-structure the customer testing process; let them use the product just as they would use it in real-life.

The project team "assumes" something will work

You know what happens when you a-s-s-u-m-e, right? Well, the rule holds true here as well. I've seen the "simplest" product features create a problem with overall product functionality just because someone didn't think they were worthwhile to test. Do the testing and avoid getting bitten in the end.

 **WARNING SIGNS**

Product testing is starting later than planned

If tasks prior to product testing are taking longer than planned and causing testing to start late, be cautious of compressing your test phases to a point where adequate product testing cannot be completed. Cutting too close to the bone on your testing means your customer will find problems later.

Your customer is finding problems that your internal project team should have found

After you've released your product to your customer group, your customer group is expecting that many of the problems in the product will be rectified and that they will be testing the product for usability. This will undoubtedly lead to frustration with your customer and reduce their faith in a stable product.

Testing is scheduled to be complete but product success criteria hasn't been met

Just because you're out of schedule doesn't mean you're done testing. I've seen one too many projects that simply stop testing their product because they have run out of time. Testing is done when the success criteria have been met, regardless of schedule.

 # TURNING IT AROUND

Pull testing back to earlier phase and re-test

If you're finding a lot of problems in your current phase of testing that should have been found in an earlier phase, consider pulling the product back to an earlier phase of testing to fix the problems and then re-releasing after the problems have been fixed.

Get the team focused on a deadline

When I've gotten into hot water during product testing, I've found it helpful to get the team focused on meeting the success criteria for the project by a certain date and putting "all hands on deck" to meet the goal. On many occasions I've temporarily changed my title from project manager to product tester to help us meet a goal.

Stop testing if there are a lot of product problems that are blocking you from continuing testing

This takes a lot of courage to do as it inevitably means a schedule slippage, but it may be required if there are too many problems in the product. Better off with a schedule slippage and a stable product than meeting schedule with a substandard product.

TAKE AWAYS

- Have a very clear definition of the different types of testing that need to be done and follow the plan
- Know what success means in your testing
- Include the customer in testing after the internal team has done their testing
- Don't assume something will work; verify it through testing

Screw-up #14

We Weren't Effective at Training the Customer

One of my favorite aspects of managing a project is doing the training. After dealing with all the details of the project and the mucky issues, I get to see the finished product in motion. I get to see excitement in my customers as they experience how the product is going to make their jobs easier. It's the part of the project where I start feeling really good about what has been developed and how it is going to be good for the customers. I just love it when it's done right.

Depending on the product produced, training the customer can be a major project component (as in technology projects) or could be a minor component (as in residential construction). If your projects don't typically focus on training the customer, feel free to skip or skim the chapter.

Developing and conducting a strong training program for your customers significantly helps in several ways:

- You drastically reduce the amount of support that your customers are going to need when the product is put into usage
- You help allay concerns and fears that the customer has about being expected to do their jobs using a new product
- You promote a positive image of the product to your customer community
- You get a final opportunity to get any product usage issues out on the table prior to releasing the product to your customers

When conducting your training, it's very important to pay attention to the little things that, while they aren't directly related to the training content, can distract from the overall training experience. On one project we spent a tremendous amount of time getting the content developed, ensuring that the training was business-based, the demos and scenarios were relevant, and all the attendees were able to get to the training class. Yet, the training was only marginally successful. Why? The room was too warm and there wasn't enough food at lunch. We focused on all the big stuff yet it was the facility that impacted the overall effectiveness of the training. Arggggh.

HOW IT HAPPENS

It's not clear who needs to be trained on what

Your training course should not be a one-size-fits-all activity where you make all your customers sit through all the training if they don't have to. When developing your training plan, make sure you've defined specifically who will require training and in what functions they will require training. It's also completely reasonable to have customers attend only specific training modules if there are some modules that are not relevant to the customer. In doing so, make sure that you involve your project customers in your training decisions so that you don't overlook some training that may be important to a customer.

The training is too product focused and doesn't put the product in context of the business and policy changes

On a recent project I managed there was significant business policy change that was being implemented by senior management that provided better context for product functionality. When we designed the training, we set aside about 30% of the training just to go through what the policy changes were, why they were implemented, and what it meant to the customers. Providing the up-front business policy and process context was crucial to understanding the end-to-end business flow and for showing how the new product fit into the business and policy changes. Had we not focused on business and policy first, much of what we did in the product wouldn't have made sense to the customers because they would have been trying to use the system under the old way of doing business, not the new way.

The project team develops the wrong type of training

Depending on your product and your organization's culture, you can take a number of different approaches to training your customers. Common methods such as instructor-led or self-paced training can be delivered via a live session, recorded for later playback, or via online real-time collaboration. When determining the best method of delivery, I like to consider the following:

- The complexity of the product
- The degree of business change that is being enforced with the implementation of the product
- The "networking" potential of getting customers together in a room
- The culture of the organization

As a general rule, my view is that the greater the complexity of the product or degree of business change that is being implemented, the greater the need for instructor-led training. There's certainly a cost trade-off to consider in that instructor-led training can be generally more expensive to conduct and is more inconvenient for the customers than doing self-paced training. This is where the consideration of some of the soft factors comes into play. In environments that I have worked, there has been tremendous value to getting people away from their desks, putting them in a room, and letting them interact on tough issues that they face. If this interaction can be beneficial to your training, consider instructor-led training. Lastly, if your organization culture has a preference toward a particular type of training, consider keeping with the culture particularly if the product complexity or degree of business change is high. The content is going to be tough enough without having to absorb a new way of being trained.

There are too many presentation slides and not enough hands-on training with the product

Imagine that I gave you an instruction manual on how to operate the navigation system in your new car two weeks before you actually got the car. You needed to read the manual but had to wait to try it out on the car. How much of that instruction manual is likely to stick with you? Probably very little. Doing training without hands-on product experience is very similar to having the navigation system instruction manual without the navigation system. Things aren't going to sink in for the customers and they're just going to try to figure things out when the product is released. After you've gotten through the business and policy changes, make heavy use of the product and let the customers use the product. They'll retain more and will be more excited about the product than if they weren't able to put the product through its paces.

The trainers understand the product, but not the business

Your credibility doesn't stop with the product. Your trainers need to be knowledgeable about the product but also need to be able to garner the respect of the customers though their understanding of the business. The best training sessions I have seen have trainers working in teams of two where one of the trainers is the project's customer team member and the other is one of the project's analysts or developers. I like to also have the project sponsor or a steering committee member kick off the training and stress the importance of the product to the business. If you have some major business or policy changes that are being implemented, it helps to have the project sponsor or a steering committee member conduct that part of the training as well.

The product keeps failing while trying to train the customers

Simply put, this is a deal killer. What the customers see during the training session is going to be what they will expect to see when the product is implemented. If the product keeps failing during training, your customers are going to walk away worrying (and telling all their peers) that they're going to be forced to use a sub-standard product.

Chances are, you're still going to be doing some testing and repairing while you're conducting training. I've had to do some training where we've needed to set expectations that some problems were still being resolved. Generally, customers were pretty amenable and didn't sweat things too much if there was an occasional problem. Just be cautious that product problems don't become the focus of attention for your audience.

 **WARNING SIGNS**

Customers aren't attending the training

If you're getting low attendance or people aren't interested in signing up for training, you're more likely to have frustrated customers that are overly critical of your solution simply because they don't understand how to use the product to make their life easier.

Trainers aren't able to address business usage issues

You can have a project team member that understands functional and technical product features, but if they don't have a good business context for how the product should be used, your customers may understand the mechanics of a product, but won't know how to apply it to their jobs.

After attending the training, customers still don't get it

So you've done the training and your customers are leaving the training confused about the product, why it is being implemented, and what it means to them. Now you have customers that are not only confused but are more likely to bad-mouth the product because they don't see the value that the product is going to provide.

 **TURNING IT AROUND**

Make the training targeted, relevant, and timely

Really understand for your different customer groups what they specifically need to use the product and the product's importance to the organization. Don't make them sit through a lot of training that is unimportant to them. Also, make sure that training is conducted close to the release date of your product.

Do a practice training session

Test your training. Do practice sessions with the project team and a small group of customers close to the process. Let people give very candid feedback on the effectiveness, relevance, and timeliness of the training. Better you practice in a safe environment than take to the tightrope for the first time without a net.

Assign your customer project team members to participate in delivering the training

Your most effective training is going to happen when the customer sees one of its own doing the training on the product. Aside from better ensuring that the product will be talked about in the context of its end usage, the customers will see that one of their peers was able to learn and master usage of the product.

Get immediate feedback on the quality of the training

Do a survey immediately following the training to make sure that the training met its objectives and that the customers feel as if they have learned what they need to know to use the product effectively.

Stop the training and re-design

If after your first couple of training sessions you see that the training just isn't being effective, contain the damage and stop the training. It may be that you only need to make some minor adjustments to make the training more effective or it could be that you have to significantly change your approach. As with testing, it takes a lot of courage to make the stop decision, but do it if a stop and re-design means a better overall product release.

 **TAKE AWAYS**

- Have a very clear training plan of who needs to be trained on what
- Train on business and policy changes first, then show how the product fits in
- Design the right type of training for your product, the environment, and the culture
- Do as much "hands-on" training as possible
- Make sure that trainers are well versed on both the business and the product
- Ensure that the product is stable prior to conducting training

Screw-up
#15

We Didn't Pull
the Plug on the
Project When
We Should Have

This book has been very focused on bringing in a project to a successful completion. But what about when a project *shouldn't* be completed? Knowing when it's time to pull the plug on a project is an important skill to build and can further cement your reputation as a project manager who is objective, credible, and rational. I've always had great respect for a project manager who was able to put the customer's interests ahead of his or her own by recommending that a project end because it was not going to meet the customer's need.

What are some key reasons you would stop a project? Here are some that I've seen:

- The anticipated benefit the project was supposed to deliver wasn't going to be realized
- The anticipated costs of the project were going to be much greater, making it cost-prohibitive
- Other projects took a higher priority due to business environment change, which meant diversion of resources from the project to other higher-priority projects
- The project's proposed design was not going to be able to meet the customer's need
- Execution of the project was going poorly and the project was unable to recover from the problems
- The change management issues on the project were too large to overcome

I think it is very important that the decision to stop a project is made by the entire project management team led by the project manager, and that there is concurrence that stopping the project is the best business decision. Whenever I stopped a project, I was very structured about reviewing with the project team the rationale for stopping the project and wanted to ensure that they were able to give feedback on the soundness of the decision. After the team agrees that stopping the project was the right decision, the team takes the recommendation to the steering committee and project sponsor for approval.

On one project where I was the project sponsor, we had as an objective to put volume discount pricing in place for a key commodity that my group purchased. Through our negotiations with our key vendors, we were very unsuccessful at getting little more than a 1-2% discount because we were unwilling to guarantee specific volumes of business to the vendor. In addition, our relationship with those vendors would have eroded because we were expecting the vendor to give a concession without us giving a similar concession. We ended up stopping the project because it just didn't make business sense for us to continue forward. Despite the fact that I was pushing very hard for us to have a volume discount structure and had a tremendous amount of passion on the issue, we agreed to stop as it was the right thing to do.

 **HOW IT HAPPENS**

There are no specific checkpoints established to ensure that the project should proceed

Earlier I discussed breaking your project up into phases that should last no longer than three months in duration. At the end of each phase, the team should assess whether the customer's needs can still be met and the cost/benefit of the project is still intact. On some projects, I have had mid-phase checkpoints to do the assessment because the information that the team would learn during that phase could have impacted the cost/benefit or customer need. The point is that you should make sure you define logical checkpoints in your project to assess whether it's in the customer's best interest to proceed.

The team is emotionally tied to the project

Earlier I discussed what can happen when your project team doesn't gel. I've seen projects, though, where the team gelled so well that they wanted the project to continue because they really enjoyed working together and were tied to "the cause." It's great when project teams work well together, but when their business objectivity becomes jaded, they're less willing to stop the project because they're having too much fun. I'm not advocating that the project team should have less fun or not bond; you just need to ensure that objectivity and sound business logic prevails.

The team relies on a silver bullet to save a sick project

Been there, done that. On one of my projects, the product that was being developed had horrendously slow performance due to some technical issues with the product. The team (at my direction) slogged away at it to try to bring the response time within acceptable limits but was unable to make things work. I brought in some additional technical expertise to help the project and they told me that I was never going to have acceptable response time with the current technical architecture. After way too much searching, I finally succumbed to pressure and we stopped the project. Doing the due-diligence on trying to rectify problems with the project is great, but don't let the problems go on too long without the hope of success.

 **WARNING SIGNS**

The customer or project sponsor loses interest in the project

If getting time with your customer or project sponsor becomes increasingly difficult, they may be losing interest due to more important priorities or lack of faith that the project is going to be completed successfully. Getting clarity from your sponsor or customer on the relative importance of the project to them is necessary in understanding whether they feel the project is still important.

The project sponsor changes

Any time you have a project sponsor change, there will likely be questions about the project, its business case, and its priority relative to other projects. The new project sponsor may have different ideas about the project and its importance relative to other ongoing or potential projects. Understanding the new project sponsor's expectations is important to knowing whether the project is on his/her radar.

There are major outstanding issues that can kill the project

Major issues that go unresolved despite efforts to address them are a strong signal that the project may be in jeopardy. Getting clarity on the true impact of the issue and the alternatives to resolving the issue will be a good guidepost on determining whether the issue has the potential to truly stop the project.

There's skepticism about the viability of the project's business case

Questions on the business case could just be an issue of educating a customer, sponsor, or stakeholder. Conversely, it could mean that the project isn't as important as it once was or that the original benefit statement is unattainable. Re-validating the project's business case is important to determine that the original business case still holds water, but you may need to take the extra step to determine if there are more important projects than your project.

 **TURNING IT AROUND**

Define checkpoint milestones to confirm project continuation

Get milestones established in the project at logical review points with your sponsor to determine whether the project still makes sense to continue. At your review points, consider going through your project continuation criteria and validating that continuing the project is still the right answer.

Assess the outstanding major issues to determine if continuing is the right answer

Get a clear understanding and diagnosis of the issues, the potential alternatives to dealing with each issue, and the courses of action that you will take under each alternative. Some of the alternatives may or may not include stopping the project.

Stop the project

If it doesn't make sense to continue the project, be deliberate about driving a stop decision with your project sponsor. Having to stop is not a fun thing to do, but it may be the best business decision.

TAKE AWAYS

- Define specific checkpoints throughout the project where you confirm that the problem statement is still valid and that you're still solving the problem
- Be the first to admit that you've got a sick project; don't let your steering committee, stakeholders or exec sponsor have to convince you of it
- Don't rely on a silver bullet to save your project

We Tripped at
the Finish Line

It's game 6 of the 1986 World Series between the New York Mets and the Boston Red Sox. The Red Sox were ahead in the series 3 games to 2 and only needed to win one more game to win the World Series. At the bottom of the ninth inning the score was tied 3-3. In the top of the tenth inning, the Red Sox scored two runs, which gave them a 5-3 lead. In the bottom of the tenth inning, the Mets came back to score two runs to even the score at 5-5. Mookie Wilson was at bat with the winning run on second base. On the tenth pitch of his at-bat, Mookie hit a routine ground ball to Bill Buckner at first base. The ball rolled between Buckner's legs into right field, which allowed the winning run to score and the Mets to win the game. The Mets then went on to win game 7 and the World Series. Now, Bill played in the majors for 22 years, had 2715 hits, and a career lifetime batting average of .289; very respectable numbers. What is he most known for, though? It's that one play in game 6.

One of the hardest screw-ups to accept on a project is when you execute well through the life of the project only to have something at the end muck things up because you claimed victory too early. I've learned (once again, through failure) that in the last few weeks of the project you must enforce very tight execution, at-least daily communication of activity status, and very quick resolution to any issues that may crop up. Don't put a blemish on your project (and potentially your career) by letting a ball roll between your legs that loses the game.

 **HOW IT HAPPENS**

Someone implements a last-minute product change that breaks something else

If you are a Monty Python fan, you may recall the comedy routine where there is a somewhat obese man who completely gorges himself on food, then, when he is offered a mint he literally explodes due to the amount of food who he ate. This is a great analogy to what can happen on a project when last-minute changes are put in the product. On a recent project where I was the business owner, I mandated to the project team during the last couple of weeks of the project that they only change the product when absolutely necessary. One of the customers convinced a developer to make an "easy" product change. The developer made the product change and broke a key feature in the product that was previously working. The "easy" change not only wasn't implemented in the final product, but precious resources were consumed implementing the change and diagnosing what happened.

Project communication among the team isn't timely

As I mentioned previously, I've found it necessary to hold very focused and regular team communications as you move into the final weeks of your project. I'm a big fan of doing daily morning meetings that focus on previous day activities, outstanding issues, and action plans for the current day. It's also super important to make sure that all the project roles are represented at the daily meetings so that everyone is able to assess activities from their own vantage point and understand how they may be affected by the day's activities. I also believe in keeping the daily meeting short, typically holding to no more than 30 minutes.

The project starts shutting down prior to completion

As a consultant, if I experienced budget pressures on a project I constantly looked at what people I could roll off of the project early to save money. This could be just good cost management if the person's activities on the project are finished, but in cases where the activities aren't completely done and the rest of the team is expected to pull up the slack, you've now created a people-resourcing risk that you didn't have beforehand. The reality is that you're most likely not saving much money (if any at all) because someone still needs to complete the activities.

WARNING SIGNS

Team members are being re-assigned to other projects

As a project nears completion, there will likely be pressure from other projects to re-assign project team members to their projects. Re-assigning some people may be in order but caution should be taken to ensure people aren't leaving too early. I have also tried to keep some project team members tethered to the project in case we needed to pull them back to help with a critical task.

Customers are demanding last-minute non-essential product changes

Whenever you hear "But this is so simple, it should only take a few minutes to complete," warning bells should be going off in your head. True, a feature change may be simple on the surface, but could be more complex when you consider other things that have to happen to ensure that the product feature is implemented correctly.

Project team communications have dropped off or are non-existent

When the project team isn't in frequent communications as the project is nearing completion, there are likely to be team missteps due to team members not understanding any last-minute issues or decisions. I prefer to err on the side of over-communicating during this time just to make sure that the team is fully aware of any developments that might affect them.

 # TURNING IT AROUND

Keep the focus

Keep the project team together, focused, and current on what is happening real-time. Make sure that the project team is aware of what things need to happen each day and who is responsible for driving key activities, issues, and decisions. Be cautious of project team members being pulled onto other projects before your project is done.

Drive the team to communicate

My preference is to have shorter, more frequent meetings at either the beginning or the end of each day to status the work to keep everyone current. On some projects I have set up a "war room" where we were able to keep current tasks, issues and decisions on whiteboards. We've even had key project team members camp in the war room so that if impromptu discussions needed to happen we had the right people assembled together to facilitate discussions.

Stabilize the product

As you get closer to product release, be very careful about implementing product changes that aren't absolutely essential to the product's functionality. Any time you introduce a change, you always stand the chance of unintentionally disturbing something that you don't mean to disturb. Don't feel obligated to fill each minute of the project with additional product features.

 TAKE AWAYS

- Avoid last-minute changes that can break something else
- Do short check-in meetings each morning to status work that needs to be done that day and monitor issues
- Don't claim victory too early; too many games have been lost in the bottom of the ninth; stay focused

The Vendor
Didn't Deliver

In the movie Jurassic Park,[1] the founder of the park, John Hammond (played by Richard Attenborough) is talking with Dennis Nedry (played by Wayne Knight) about the security system that Nedry developed for the park. In the dialogue, Hammond and Nedry are arguing about Nedry's work and the financials of the contract. The dialogue goes something like this:

NEDRY: I am totally unappreciated in my time. We can run the whole park from this room, with minimal staff, for up to three days. You think that kind of automation is easy? Or cheap? You know anybody who can network eight Connection Machines and de-bug two million lines of code for what I bid this job? Because I'd sure as hell like to see them try.

HAMMOND: I'm sorry about your financial problems. I really am. But they are your problems.

NEDRY: You're right, John. You're absolutely right. Everything's my problem.

HAMMOND: I will not get drawn into another financial conversation with you, Dennis. I really will not.

NEDRY: I don't think there's been any debate. There's no debate...my mistakes....

HAMMOND: I don't blame people for their mistakes, but I do ask that they pay for them.

So, let's dig deeper into what's going on here. The customer (Hammond) is clearly irritated with the performance and results that he is seeing from the vendor (Nedry) and intends to hold the vendor to the original terms of the deal. The vendor is clearly irritated with the customer because the customer is focused on what hasn't been done and doesn't show appreciation or empathy for the vendor's completed work or financial situation. Both parties are clearly exhausted with the arrangement and will in the highest likelihood never do business again.

Look beyond the unrealistic premise of the movie (a man uses dinosaurs created from DNA harvested from a million-year-old bug to build an enterprising tourist theme park) to key points in this very brief but realistic piece of dialogue:

- Vendor didn't perform
- Customer gets ticked
- Vendor gets ticked
- Customer digs in heels
- Vendor gets even more ticked
- Customer digs in even more
- Vendor gets eaten by hungry carnivores (OK, the eaten part may not be completely realistic)

I've been on both sides of this net enough to know that when you get into a situation like that, both parties are going to lose. The vendor loses credibility, profitability on the current contract, revenue on potential future contracts, and gains poor references for other projects both inside and outside of the customer's company. The customer loses time and money in that their product is incomplete, non-existent, or later than planned. Regardless of whose fault it is, the project has failed, and something that the customer was counting on to help them do something better than they had before is now not going to happen within the timeframe they wanted it.

 **HOW IT HAPPENS**

The vendor oversells their product or capabilities

From the customer side of the table, I only need to see a vendor attempt to oversell their products or capabilities once to get a negative impression of them. When assessing products, I very much want to see the actual product in action mirroring our actual work environment to the best extent possible being demonstrated by people who understand the intricacies of the product. If you have developed a requirements checklist to evaluate the product, have each requirement demonstrated so you can get a good context of how that requirement will be satisfied by the system. This may seem tedious, but the time is better spent up front to understand how the product performs and give you good visibility as to what requirements will and won't be met by the product.

When assessing services, I am very focused on the experience of the team and the other projects that they have done before which may be similar to the work that we are doing. Meeting key project team members prior to making a decision has always been a critical factor in making a vendor choice. I've had it both ways: sometimes a vendor that was the favorite ended up not being chosen because they didn't bring in key project team members or brought in people who didn't have the necessary experience and skills to get the job done. Other times, a runner-up vendor ended up winning the work because of the people who were going to do the work.

There isn't a clear agreement on what the vendor is supposed to do

This all goes back to a crisp, clear, and well-communicated statement of work. It's very easy to dismiss this work as "contract administrivia" because both parties want to get going on the project. I've been on many projects where the contract and statement of work was completed well after work had started. Sometimes you can get lucky and not run into problems, but in my book, why add one more risk to the project that can be completely mitigated?

The customer doesn't live up to their obligations

Most times when we think about the vendor not performing, we may assume that the vendor had complete control over the variables affecting their non-performance. What about the situation where the customer was supposed to be providing something that they didn't provide? As a consultant, I have been on several projects where the terms of the agreement between us and the customer required that specific customer resources were to participate on the project on a full-time basis, yet the customer did not live up to their part of the deal. We ended up having to bring in additional resources to the project at an additional cost to the customer. Despite the fact that we were able to recover, it created a fire drill and caused us to have to do unplanned work on the project to secure the additional resources.

The vendor does a "bait and switch" with resources

With most proposals that have a service component, you may see resumes of subject matter experts who will participate in some form on the project. I would expect that the vendor would be putting their best foot forward in demonstrating that they have the skills and capabilities to ensure success. Where things can go awry, though, is when the resources that actually work on the project differ from those that are contained in the proposal. Sometimes, the switched resources are capable and can do the work, but my radar goes up when the resources that actually show up are different from the resources that I was expecting. If the vendor does not provide advanced notification of changes in key resources and you question the capabilities of the switched resources, you should consider immediately stopping the affected pieces of work and resolve the issue right away. As a project manager, I have been burned a couple of times by an inexperienced vendor resource being brought onto a project and not delivering what we expected them to do.

The vendor isn't treated like part of the team

When the project starts and the team begins forming, leave your business cards at the door and *be one team*. On one project I managed as the project sponsor, we had at peak 50 people from five different companies across a dozen countries working on the project. To top it off, we did the project in five months at breakneck pace. Despite the fact that we had four different vendors that typically compete with each other working on the project, we immediately set a tone on the project that we succeeded or failed as one team and that it didn't matter who worked for which company. The bottom line is that we delivered a functioning product, process, and infrastructure that was praised as a huge success by our customers and management. In conducting our post-mortem with the entire project team, everyone agreed that, while the project was very aggressive and that people worked a lot of hours, the teaming across the different companies was hugely successful and it was one of the best projects that they ever worked on. I can honestly say that throughout the project not once was there any finger pointing between companies and I never saw any gamesmanship amongst the vendors to one-up each other.

The vendor is over- or under-managed by the project manager

Depending on the type of arrangement you have with the vendor, your degree of management of that vendor can vary significantly. Management could be to a set of very high-level milestones or could be just managing hourly activities of vendor resources. Wherever your agreement falls, it's important that you know where your level of management starts and stops and that you manage within those bounds of accountability. When you under-manage the vendor, the vendor is not getting the degree of guidance expected and will likely miss some things that are necessary for project completion. When you over-manage the vendor, you are now dis-empowering the vendor and have by default taken responsibility for work that the vendor was supposed to do. In either situation, the vendor's ability to deliver successfully is hampered by either lack of direction or too much direction.

 # WARNING SIGNS

The vendor keeps slipping their scheduled dates

Occasional minor schedule slips can be tolerated; it's the chronic date slips that erode trust in the vendor's ability to deliver. Compound the situation with a vendor that not only delivers late, but also delivers a sub-standard product to boot and you've got a major problem on your hands.

The vendor is rolling people off of the project earlier than anticipated

If the vendor is under cost pressure you may see them getting very aggressive in rolling some of their people off of the project to help keep their costs down. This will mean that the rest of the project team will have to pick up the slack for the lost resources and can likely result in both a scheduling slip and reduced quality of the product.

The vendor spends time trying to sell additional work using their project team members

The vendor most likely will be eager to do more work with you and may be looking for additional projects to work on with your organization. I understood that vendors I worked with were in business to sell work, but I required that they couldn't defocus the people assigned to the project to help sell more work while the project was in progress.

The vendor's deliverables aren't meeting your expectations

It's possible that the vendor's deliverable is sub-standard; it also could be possible that you are not communicating your deliverable expectations effectively and the vendor is left to guessing what you want. The vendor may or may not understand what is expected of them on a specific deliverable or simply may not be capable of producing the deliverable.

The vendor has staffed the project with inexperienced people

I have seen quite a few projects where the vendor personnel assigned to the project were put in roles that frankly were well beyond "stretch assignments." They were simply over their head in what they were trying to do. I've seen some survive, but I've also seen some projects get into major trouble because the staff was too inexperienced to do the work.

TURNING IT AROUND

Address the people skill sets issue

If the vendor's project team members don't have the right skills to do the project, ask that they be replaced with people with skill sets that better fit project need. If they can't replace the people, you probably need to replace the vendor.

Manage to more detailed, frequent milestones

If your vendor is having difficulty meeting schedule milestones, try managing to more detailed, frequent milestones to see if that helps. Ultimately, you probably shouldn't need to micro-manage the vendor to detailed delivery milestones, but you may need to do so to get you through the project.

Contain the vendor

If your vendor is out scoping for additional work and neglecting your project, rein them in and keep them focused on delivery of your project. One approach I've used is to agree to endorse them for other projects only after our project was done. My endorsement was contingent on their work product meeting expectations, being delivered on time and within budget.

Make sure that the vendor has skin in the game

Have clear acceptance or performance criteria established up front with the vendor. Ensure that the vendor's compensation is tied to the project's success criteria to keep the vendor and the project team's goals in sync.

Replace the vendor

If the vendor isn't going to cut the mustard, be deliberate in replacing them. When you do this, just make sure that the vendor was the source of the problem. If another vendor comes in with qualified credentials and you have the same problems, the problem may not be with the vendor, it may be with the project team or you as the project manager.

 **TAKE AWAYS**

- Make sure that the vendor is capable of delivering what is agreed-upon and staffs the project appropriately.
- Meet the people who are actually going to do the work and get a clear understanding of how they are planning to do the project, their reservations with the project, and what they think the project will need to succeed.
- Have a clear, concise, and relevant statement of work that outlines clear success criteria and milestones for the project.

- Make sure that the vendor feels and behaves like part of the team, including sharing in the successes and failures.
- Manage the vendor per the statement of work and avoid over or under-managing the work.

[1] Copyright 2004 by Universal Studios. Courtesy of Universal Studios Publishing Rights, a division of Universal Studios Licensing LLLP. All Rights Reserved.

We Had No Fallback Position in Case the Product Failed

One winter my family was visiting my wife's parents in a small town in Arizona. My father-in-law took me out to an open airfield where a group of men were flying radio-controlled (RC) airplanes. I was amazed at the beauty and deftness at which these men were able to takeoff, fly, land, and avoid crashing into other planes. One of the pilots asked me if I was interested in taking a hand at the radio controls. He then handed me a radio control that was tethered to a master controller that he operated. With his master control, he was able to give me control and take it away in case I got into trouble. I humored him and let him have the master controls thinking that once we got off the ground I could just take over from there and wouldn't need his help. Well, he got off the ground just fine, got into open airspace, and asked me if I was ready to take control. I replied, "Roger" (even though his name was Bill) and he gave me control. I had control for about two seconds and the plane started into a nosedive, whereupon he said "taking control" and cut off my controls. This went on for what seemed like hours; him giving me control, me tanking the plane, and him saying "Taking control" and cutting off my controls. I learned a new respect for radio controlled airplane enthusiasts that day and was thankful for Bill protecting me from myself.

The common thread between this story and project management is having a contingency plan in case something goes wrong. In my RC experience, I had someone with master controls who was able to take over whenever there was trouble. In implementing a new product, having a contingency plan in case something goes wrong is just good prudent planning. In thinking through contingency positions, let's first get into some common implementation approaches:

- **"Big Bang"**—This approach is used when you are going to convert an entire population over from an old product to a new product. It generally carries the most risk since everyone is converted at the same time and the magnitude of business interruption can be significant if a problem occurs.

- **Phased**—This approach is used when you can break up your population into logical groupings and you convert groups within the population over in a phased approach. When using this approach, the first group to convert may also be called the "pilot" group; subsequent groups will be converted after the pilot group is deemed as acceptable.

- **Parallel**—This approach carries the least amount of risk but is also the most expensive approach because you ask customers to do their job twice; once using the old product and once using the new product, until the customer is comfortable with the new product. After that, the old product is retired.

Over the years, I generally preferred to do phased product implementations as it reduced the risk of significant business interruption and allowed us to work out any problems using a smaller population. There were times, though, when I did not have the luxury of a phased implementation and had to do a big bang implementation because something needed to be implemented quickly. Under both approaches, having a strong contingency plan was critical to ensuring that the team knew what they had to do if something went wrong and in securing the confidence of the customers and the product sponsor that the risk of business interruption would be minimized.

The best contingency plans I have seen very clearly outline possible problem scenarios and clear courses of action should the problem scenario come true. The most important thing with the contingency plan is to gain agreement among team members, key stakeholders, and the product sponsor on what action will be taken for different problems. Recall earlier in this book when I talk about risk management. In managing to contingencies, all that the project manager is doing is managing risks in a very tight, concise, intense timeframe and knowing what needs to be done should any of the risks come true. It is also during this time that the calmness and prescriptiveness of the project manager is paramount. The project manager's job during the contingency management process is to keep a cool head, stick with the plan, and ensure that the right people are involved in any contingency plan decisions.

HOW IT HAPPENS

There is no contingency plan in place

This to me is like juggling chainsaws. If everything works out fine and the juggler catches the right end every time, he wows the crowd and may get a shot at being on late-night television. If there's one mistake, though, the juggler's juggling days are over and he is off to learn a new trade. If you have no contingency plan in place with courses of action for business failure scenarios and one of the scenarios comes true, people will be making decisions out of haste and are likely to miss something.

There is a contingency plan, but it isn't followed

This is very similar to not following a project plan. The project manager could develop a great contingency plan and then put it in a desk drawer never to see light of day again. As a project manager, you need the discipline to keep people on plan and keep people calm when there are bombs going off left and right.

Project management does not stay engaged through the implementation

It's my opinion that the project manager's job doesn't stop once the product is released to the customer. My view is that it's crucial that the project manager stay engaged through the implementation until the point that the customer is comfortable with using the new product. If the project manager disengages too soon, managing the contingency plan is left up to chance and poor decisions are likely to be made.

 **WARNING SIGNS**

The customer is asking questions about what happens if the new product implementation isn't successful

When your customer is asking "what if" questions, that's a good indication that the plan either isn't complete or the plan hasn't been communicated well to customers. Many of the customers that I have worked with don't get a thrill by swinging on a trapeze without a safety net. They need to feel comfortable that their business will not experience undue interruption because of a poor product release.

The project team doesn't know what it needs to do in the event of an unsuccessful implementation

When you have to implement a contingency plan, the project team will need to be clear on what its role is in executing a smooth contingency plan. When the project team is confused about what its role is in the contingency plan, there will likely be mistakes and further customer interruption as the project team figures out what it needs to do.

 # TURNING IT AROUND

Get the contingency plan scenarios down

Get a clear understanding on what the possible failure scenarios might be with the product, review the failure scenarios with the project team and the customer and then develop the contingency plan based on each failure. For each failure, make sure that each team member knows what they need to do so that recovery will be swift and the team members won't spend time trying to figure out what they're supposed to do.

Test the plan

Depending on the mission-critical nature of your product, you may want to run a test of the contingency plan to ensure that it will work. At a minimum, make sure that the business and the project team are clear on what needs to be done in the event of failure.

Go back to the old product, fix the new, and then re-release

In the unfortunate event that your product release fails, be very deliberate about the decision to invoke the contingency plan and implement it. Communicate very clearly to the customers, letting them know that the contingency plan is being invoked and what they can expect under the plan. Clear, crisp, and frequent communication during this time is critical. If you "go dark" on communication then you're likely to feed the rumor mill on the stability of the product and erode confidence in the new product and your ability to deliver it.

TAKE AWAYS

- Have a clear contingency plan in place that outlines potential failure scenarios and know when to pull the trigger on implementing the contingency plan.
- Make the best effort to define a manageable scope for your initial implementation.
- Stay engaged! Success can only be declared once the customers are operating steady state with the new product.

Wrapping it up...

OK, so you either skipped to the last chapter or you made it through the book. My sincere hope is that you were able to highlight a few key nuggets in this book that will help you make your current or future projects more successful. I also hope that this book doesn't become a shelf ornament in your office that never gets opened again. My hope is that you refer back to the book again and again and that it is helpful to you in years to come. To supplement this book, I will maintain some additional resources and templates on www.projectmanagementadvisor.com. Check back to the website frequently as I will continue to add information to help you better succeed as a project manager.

Let me leave you with just a few closing thoughts:

- Remember that your role as a project manager is similar to conducting an orchestra; your responsibility is to make sure that all the project resources work together as harmoniously as possible. Make beautiful music with them.
- While you may not always make decisions that are popular, make sure that your decisions are best for the project and the business. You may not always win a popularity contest; you will be respected for doing the right thing.
- Have some fun and don't forget to laugh along the way. Project teams that are able to share some fun or have a laugh together will hold up much better during tough times. Let your project team see your human side; the tone you set will pervade through the project team.

Now go drive that project to success!

Index

A

actions on problems, 101
  prepared reports concise, 101
  problem warnings, 102-103
  solutions to problems, 103-104
  team meetings not held, 100
  tracking schedule, 100
actuals spent, 85
adding product features, 109
  controlling, 108
  problem warnings, 109-110
  setting appropriately, 108
  solutions to problems, 110-111
addressing incorrect problem, 6
  communication plans, 73-74
  cost management problems, 89-90
  customer training, 127-128
  design problems, 19
  finishing failures, 139
  knowing when to stop, 134
  progress reporting, 103-104
  project schedule issues, 37-38
  scope, 110-111
  sponsorship problems, 46-47
  stakeholder problems, 63-64
  technology issues, 28
  testing, 119
  vendor issues, 148-149
adjustments, 6
  defining, 3-4
  displaying, 6
  organizing priorities, 4-5
  poorly articulated, 2-3
assumptions of success, 117
  customer included, 117
  plan inexistent, 115-116
  plan not followed, 116
  problem warnings, 118

solutions to problems, 119
success definition, 116
audience definition, 71
  delivery personnel, 72
  ignoring plan, 71
  matrix, 69-70
  plan development, 68-70
  problem warnings, 72-73
  project sponsors, 43-44
  solutions, 73-74
  stakeholders, 63
  targeting audience, 71-72
  timely, 137
automated processes, inefficiencies,
    16-17
  customers, 13-16
  incorrect scope, 10-13
  poor change process, 17-18
  poor timing, 14-15
  problem warnings, 18-19
  solutions, 19

B

Big Bang approach, contingency
    plans, 153
budgets
  contingency funds, 85
  request additional funding,
      87-88
  resource mix, 86
    additional funding, 87-88
    contingency fund, 86-87
    estimate at completion not man-
        aged, 86
    problem warnings, 88-89
    solutions to problems, 89-90
    versus actual, 86

C

communications, 69-70
  audience definition, 71
  delivery personnel, 72
  ignoring plan, 71
  matrix, 69-70
  problem warnings, 72-73
  solutions, 73-74
  targeting audience, 71-72
contingency funds
  unknown consumption, 88
  unmanaged, 86-87
contingency plans, 152-154
  clear definition, 61-64
  confusion about problem, 5
    member reassignment, 137
    staying focused, 5
  customers, 13-16, 35-37, 42-47, 100
  none in place, 154
  problem warnings, 155
  project management not engaged,
    155
  solutions to problems, 156
cost management
  budgeted resource mix, 86
  current variance keeps growing, 88
  estimate at completion not man-
    aged, 86
  request additional funding, 87-88
  unknown contingencies, 88
  unmanaged contingency funds,
    86-87
  unplanned work, 88
  variance fluctuations, 89
current budgets, 85
current variances, 85
  fluctuations, 89
  keeps growing, 88
customers
  clarity of who is trained, 123
    context, 123
    hands-on product experience,125
    method of delivery, 124
    problem solutions, 127-128
    product failure, 126
    trainers don't understand busi-
      ness, 125
    warning problems, 126-127
  design, 13-20
  inadequate design involvement,
    13-14
  meeting design requirements, 15-16
  obligations not met, 144
    oversell products, 143-144
    poor management by project
      manager, 146

  resources switched, 145
  solutions to problems,
    148-149
  statement of work not
    clear, 144
  treatment as team, 145-146
  warning problems, 147-148
prepared reports concise, 101
project schedule solutions, 37
project schedule understanding, 35
roles, 50-56
stakeholders, 61
training, 123-127
weekly status meetings, 100

D

design phase, 14-15
  automated process inefficiencies,
    16-17
  changes late in project, 19
  customers, 10-20
  defining, 71, 76
    identifying, 68
    lack of defining, 78-79
    management actions not
      taken, 80
    no mitigation strategies, 79
    solutions, 81-82
    targeting, 71-72
    warning of issues, 80-81
  dependency solutions, 37-38
  detail inconsistencies, 32-38, 100
  incorrect designs, 10-13
  obligation to vendor not
    met, 144
  poor change process, 17
  stakeholders, 60-64
  timing, design phase, 14-15
  training, 122-128
detail inconsistency, designs, 32-33
  duration length, 34-35
  problem warnings, 36-37
  project team understanding, 35
  solutions to problems, 37-38
  task deliverables, 35
  task dependencies, 34

E

ETC (estimate to complete), 85-86,
  89, 94
emotional tie to project, 131
  no checkpoints, 131
  problem warnings, 132-133
  recovery not possible, 132
  solution to problems, 134

estimate to complete (ETC), 85-86, 89, 94
experience level, 54-55

F-G

failures, finishing
  customer demands last-minute, 138
  last-minute changes, 136
  problem warnings, 138
  solutions to problems, 139
  team communications failing, 138
  team reassignment, 137-138
  timely communications, 137
fallback positions
  contingency plan not followed, 154
  customer question success, 155
  none in place, 154
  project management not engaged, 155
  project team confusion, 155
finishing failures
  last-minute changes, 136
  last-minute customer demands, 138
  team communications failing, 138
  team reassignment, 137-138
  timely communications, 137

H-I

halting project, 131-133

incorrect perception of issues
  clearly defining problem, 3-4
  during design, 10-13, 20
  mission statement, 2-3
  priorities unorganized, 4-5
  solutions, 6
  warning signs, 5-6
inefficiencies, 16-17
issues
  defining, 76
  incorrect perception of, 2-6
  lack of definition, 78-79
  management, 76-82
  management actions not taken, 80
  no mitigation strategies, 79
  project management not engaged, 155
  solutions, 81-82
  warnings, 80-81

J-L

knowing when to stop project, 131

last-minute changes, 136
  problem warnings, 138

solutions to problems, 139
  team reassignment, 137
  timely communications, 137
lack of management, 86-87

M-N

member reassignment, 137
  none in place, 154-156
  not clear to vendor, 144
  not managed, 86
mission statements
  adjustments, 6
  defining, 3-4
  displaying, 6
  organizing priorities, 4-5
  poorly articulated, 2-3
mitigation plans, issue management, 80

O-P

organization, 4-5
oversells, 143-144

parallel approach, contingency plans, 153
phased approach, contingency plans, 153
problem warnings, 88-89
  request additional funding, 87-88
  solutions to problems, 89-90
progress, 92-100
  actions on problems, 101
  prepared reports concisely, 101
  problem warnings, 102-103
  solutions to problems, 103-104
  reports, 100-104
  team meeting not held, 100
  tracking schedule, 100
project schedules, 35
  detail inconsistency, 32-33
  duration length, 34-35
  problem warnings, 27-28
  project team understanding, 35
  selection problems, 24-26
  solutions, 28, 37-38
  task deliverables, 35
  task dependencies, 34
project tasks, failure to get done, 36-37
project teams, 5, 35
Project Management Advisor, 159

R

remaining budgets, 85
remaining contingency funds, 85

reports
  actions on problems, 101
  no resolution ownership, 102
  prepared reports concise, 101
  project team problem confusion, 102
  requests for status, 102
  surprise problems, 102
  team meetings not held, 100
  tracking progress, 104
  tracking schedule, 100
  updating schedules, 103
resource mix, budgeted *versus* actual, 86
risks
  defining, 81-82
  lack of defining, 78-79
  list not in place, 80
  management, 79
  management actions not taken, 80
  mitigation plan, 80
  no mitigation strategies, 79
roles
  clear definition, 50-51
  confusion, 55
  deliverable accountability, 53
  milestone celebration, 55
  problem solutions, 56-57
  project manager experience level, 54-55
  rallying cry, 52
  unproductive discussions, 51-52, 56
  unsupportive of members, 56

S

schedules
  detail inconsistency, 32-33
  duration length, 34-35
  project team understanding, 35
  solutions to problems, 37-38
  task deliverables, 35
  task dependencies, 34
scopes
  adding product features, 109
  confusion, 110
  controlling, 108
  incorrect during design, 10-13
  setting appropriately, 108
  staying focused, 20
  team overtime, 109
shipping dates slipping, 147
sponsorships
  communications with, 43-44
  decision-making authority, 42
  difficulty finding, 5

  meetings, 44
  problem warnings, 45
  solutions to issues, 46-47
  use of steering committee, 42
stakeholders, 60
  clear definition, 61
  identifying problem personnel, 62
  involving appropriate personnel, 61-62
  problem warnings, 62-63
  solutions, 63-64
status reports
  actions on problems, 101
  no resolution ownership, 102
  prepared reports concise, 101
  project team problem confusion, 102
  request for status, 102
  surprise problems, 102
  team meetings not held, 100
  tracking, 100-104
  updating schedule, 103
steering committees, when to use, 42
stopping project
  change in sponsor, 133
  emotional tie to project, 131
  no checkpoints, 131
  outstanding issues, 133
  project skepticism, 133
  recovery not possible, 132
  sponsor loses interest, 132
suppliers, stakeholders, 61

T

tasks
  deliverables, 35
  failure to get done, 36-37
teams
  accountability, 53
  celebration, 55
  clear definition, 50-51
  confusion, 5, 55
  deliverable accountability, 53
  milestone celebration, 55
  problem solutions, 56-57
  project manager experience level, 54-55
  project understanding, 35
  rallying cry, 52
  roles, 50-57
  staying focused, 5
  unproductive discussions, 51-52, 56
  unsupportive of members, 56
technologies, 28
  customer complaints, 27
  failure rates, 27

problem solutions, 28
selection problems, 24-26
tests
  assumptions of success, 117
  customer finding problems, 118
  customer included, 117
  plan inexistent, 115-116
  plan not followed, 116
  success criteria not met, 118
  success definition, 116
  timing, 118
timing, design phase, 14-15
total budgets, 85
training
  attendance, 126
  business usage issues, 126
  clarity of who is trained, 123
  confusion following training, 127
  context, 123
  hands-on product experience, 125
  method of delivery, 124
  product failure, 126
  trainers don't understand
    business, 125

U-Z

vendors
  customer obligation not met, 144
  inexperienced staff, 148
  oversell products, 143-144
  poor management by project manager, 146
  resources switched, 145
  rolling people off project, 147
  selling more work, 147
  shipping dates slipping, 147
  statement of work not clear, 144
  substandard deliverables, 148
  treatment as team, 145-146

SYMPTOMS INDEX

automated processes, inefficiencies, 16-17
  customers, 13-16
  incorrect scope, 10-13
  poor change process, 17-18
  poor timing, 14-15
  problem warnings, 18-19
  solutions, 19
budgets, request additional funding, 87-88
communications
  audience definition, 71
  delivery personnel, 72

ignoring plan, 71
matrix, 69-70
problem warnings, 72-73
solutions, 73-74
targeting audience, 71-72
contingency funds
  unknown consumption, 88
  unmanaged, 86-87
cost management
  budgeted resource mix, 86
  current variance keeps growing, 88
  estimate at completion not managed, 86
  request additional funding, 87-88
  unknown contingencies, 88
  unmanaged contingency funds, 86-87
  unplanned work, 88
  variance fluctuations, 89
current variances
  fluctuations, 89
  keeps growing, 88
customers
  design, 13-20
  training, 123-127
designs
  automated process inefficiencies, 16-17
  changes late in project, 19
  customers, 10-20
  incorrect, 10-13
  poor change process, 17
  timing, design phase, 14-15
estimate to complete (ETC), 94
  fluctuations, 89
  not managed, 86
failures,finishing
  last-minute changes, 136

  last-minute customer demands, 138
  team communications failing, 138
  team reassignment, 137-138
  timely communications, 137
fallback positions
  contingency plan not followed, 154
  customer question success, 155
  none in place, 154
automated processes, inefficiencies, 16-17
  customers, 13-16
  incorrect scope, 10-13
  poor change process, 17-18

poor timing, 14-15
problem warnings, 18-19
solutions, 19
budgets, request additional funding,
    87-88
communications
    audience definition, 71
    delivery personnel, 72
    ignoring plan, 71
    matrix, 69-70
    problem warnings, 72-73
    solutions, 73-74
    targeting audience, 71-72
contingency funds
    unknown consumption, 88
    unmanaged, 86-87
cost management
    budgeted resource mix, 86
    current variance keeps
        growing, 88
    estimate at completion not man-
        aged, 86
    request additional funding,
        87-88
    unknown contingencies, 88
    unmanaged contingency funds,
        86-87
    unplanned work, 88
    variance fluctuations, 89
current variances
    fluctuations, 89
    keeps growing, 88
customers
    design, 13-20
    training, 123-127
designs
    automated process inefficiencies,
        16-17
    changes late in project, 19
    customers, 10-20
    incorrect, 10-13
    poor change process, 17
    timing, design phase, 14-15
estimate to complete (ETC), 94
    fluctuations, 89
    not managed, 86
failures,finishing
    last-minute changes, 136
    last-minute customer
        demands, 138
    team communications
        failing, 138
    team reassignment, 137-138
    timely communications, 137
fallback positions
    contingency plan not

followed, 154
    customer question success, 155
    none in place, 154
    project management not
        engaged, 155
    project team confusion, 155
finishing failures
    last-minute changes, 136
    last-minute customer
        demands, 138
    team communications
        failing, 138
    team reassignment, 137-138
    timely communications, 137
issue management, 76-82
    defining, 81-82
    lack of defining, 78-79
    list not in place, 80
    management actions not
        taken, 80
    mitigation plan, 80
    no mitigation strategies, 79
mission statements
    adjustments, 6
    defining, 3-4
    displaying, 6
    organizing priorities, 4-5
    poorly articulated, 2-3
mitigation plans, issue manage-
    ment, 80
progress reports
    actions on problems, 101
    no resolution ownership, 102
    prepared reports concise, 101
    project team problem
        confusion, 102
    requests for status, 102
    surprise problems, 102
    team meetings not held, 100
    tracking progress, 104
    tracking schedule, 100
    updating schedules, 103
project schedules
    detail inconsistency, 32-33
    duration length, 34-35
    project team understanding, 35
    solutions to problems, 37-38
    task deliverables, 35
    task dependencies, 34
project tasks, failure to get done,
    36-37
project teams, 5, 35
reports, progress, 100-104
resource mix, budgeted *versus* actu-
    al, 86
risks, 76

defining, 81-82
lack of defining, 78-79
list not in place, 80
management actions not taken, 80
mitigation plan, 80
no mitigation strategies, 79
schedules
detail inconsistency, 32-33
duration length, 34-35
project team understanding, 35
solutions to problems, 37-38
task deliverables, 35
task dependencies, 34
scope
adding product features, 109
confusion, 110
controlling, 108
incorrect during design, 10-13
setting appropriately, 108
staying focused, 20
team overtime, 109
shipping dates slipping, 147
sponsorships
communications with, 43-44
decision-making authority, 42
difficulty finding, 5
meetings, 44
problem warnings, 45
solutions to issues, 46-47
use of steering committee, 42
stakeholders
clear definition, 61
identifying problem personnel, 62
involving appropriate personnel, 61-62
problem warnings, 62-63
solutions, 63-64
status reports
actions on problems, 101
no resolution ownership, 102
prepared reports concise, 101
project team problem confusion, 102
request for status, 102
surprise problems, 102
team meetings not held, 100
tracking, 100-104
updating schedule, 103
steering committees, when to use, 42
stopping project
change in sponsor, 133
emotional tie to project, 131
no checkpoints, 131

outstanding issues, 133
project skepticism, 133
recovery not possible, 132
sponsor loses interest, 132
tasks
deliverables, 35
failure to get done, 36-37
teams
confusion about problem, 5
project understanding, 35
roles, 50-57
staying focused, 5
technologies
customer complaints, 27
failure rates, 27
problem solutions, 28
selection problems, 24-26
tests
assumptions of success, 117
customer finding problems, 118
customer included, 117
plan inexistent, 115-116
plan not followed, 116
success criteria not met, 118
success definition, 116
timing, 118
timing, design phase, 14-15
training
business usage issues, 126
clarity of who is trained, 123
confusion following training, 127
context, 123
hands-on product experience, 125
method of delivery, 124
product failure, 126
trainers don't understand business, 125
training attendance, 126
vendors
customer obligation not met, 144
inexperienced staff, 148
oversell products, 143-144
poor management by project manager, 146
resources switched, 145
rolling people off project, 147
selling more work, 147
shipping dates slipping, 147
statement of work not clear, 144
substandard deliverables, 148
treatment as team, 145-146

The Definitive Guide to Project Management

The Definitive Guide to Project Management will show you, step by step, how to deliver the right projects in the right way at the right time, while maintaining your life balance. Using the principles of both traditional and critical chain project management, the authors help you master the essentials of good project management and then explore the situations where good projects and good business meet. How to manage risks and politics; how to demonstrate the value added by a project; how to communicate upwards and downwards in project teams; how to energize projects; how to turn failing projects around; and how to spot likely problem projects. As well as covering all the conceptual tools needed for project management, this book pays special attention to the soft issues involved — how to manage the people side of project management.

ISBN 0273663976, © 2004, 256 pp., $19.95

The Project Workout, Third Edition

This uniquely interactive book takes the reader step-by-step through project management, acting as a valuable executive companion for delivering successful projects and managing portfolios to drive a business forward. This third edition of the definitive book on business-led program and project management offers help at every stage, from building a project team to reaping the rewards of a timely and successful project. It is a valuable companion for project managers and executives at any level, and a comprehensive resource for students of project management. Projects are an important strategic management tool and a way of life for every businessperson. But how do you get started and ensure a successful outcome? This book takes the reader step-by-step through project management, acting as a companion and guide to ultimate project success.

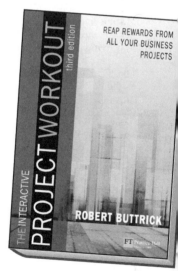

ISBN 0273681818, © 2005, 512 pp., $27.95